R.I.P.

[*Read in Peace*]

This book is dedicated to:

_____

halloween

boo!

ISBN-13: 978-0-8487-3391-9
ISBN-10: 0-8487-3391-6
Library of Congress Control Number: 2009941581
Printed in the United States of America
First Printing 2010

Oxmoor House
VP, Publishing Director: Jim Childs
Editorial Director: Susan Payne Dobbs
Brand Manager: Terri Laschober Robertson
Senior Editor: Rebecca Brennan
Managing Editor: Laurie S. Herr

Gooseberry Patch Halloween
Editor: Katherine Cobbs
Project Editor: Emily Chappell
Director, Test Kitchens: Elizabeth Tyler Austin
Assistant Director, Test Kitchens: Julie Christopher
Test Kitchens Professionals: Allison E. Cox, Julie Gunter,
Kathleen Royal Phillips, Catherine Crowell Steele,
    Ashley T. Strickland
Photography Director: Jim Bathie
Senior Photo Stylist: Kay E. Clarke
Associate Photo Stylist: Katherine Eckert Coyne
Senior Production Manager: Greg A. Amason

Contributors
Designer: Carol Damsky
Layout Design: Maya Metz Logue
Copy Editor: Jasmine Hodges
Proofreader: Adrienne Davis
Interns: Sarah Bélanger, Georgia Dodge, Perri K. Hubbard
Photographer: Becky Luigart-Stayner
Photo Stylists: Melanie Clarke, Mindi Shapiro

To order additional publications, call 1-800-765-6400.
For more books to enrich your life, visit **oxmoorhouse.com**
To search, savor, and share thousands of recipes, visit
myrecipes.com

Dear Friend,

Halloween is one of America's favorite holidays and one of ours at Gooseberry Patch too! We can't help but get carried away with all the fun. Whether it's carving, painting or embellishing pumpkins, hanging cobwebs or adding spooky touches around the house. Take a peek at our inspirational decorating ideas on beginning on page 28 for bright and cheery or downright devilish ways to pay homage to Halloween!

Let the fun last all month long with our enticing party ideas. Invite the neighbors to fill up at a Spooktacular Block Party (page 58) before heading out for a night of trick-or-treating. Make-ahead main dishes like Don't-Be-a-Chicken Chili and Mummy Hot Dogs are a treat for busy cooks and will delight goblins of all ages yet keep the cook sane. Show a scary movie every weekend in October by hosting a Fright Night Film Festival (page 92). Serve inspired theater snacks (page 94) like Harvest Moon Popcorn and Campfire Corn Dogs. For a devilish good time with adults in mind, throw a Masquerade Party and serve tasty finger foods in creepy disguise like Monster Eyes (page 76), a savory bite that at first glance gives a fright, and Munchable Mice (page 80), a chocolate-cherry treat that looks like it squeaks.

When time is ticking, never fear, we bring you great ideas for treats and eats easily made on the fly (broom not necessary)! Flip through our Quick Tricks section (page 162) to get fast and easy ideas for virtually everything under the full moon. Need someone to hold your hand? Our Gooseberry Grab Bag (page 178) is chock-full of patterns and stencils to inspire and guide.

So take a look inside, little pretties...if you dare...for lots of hair-raising how-tos and whimsical ideas perfect for raising spirits this Halloween.

From our frighteningly fun family to yours,

Vickie & JoAnn

contents

INTRODUCTION

Letter from Vickie and Jo Ann   5

CHAPTERS

1   Pumpkin Parade   8
     if you carve it, they will come

2   Devilish Décor   28
     for raising spirits

3   Ghoulish Gatherings   46
     recipes for a spooktacular time

4   Tantalizing Treats   128
     so you won't get tricked

5   Fiendish Fun   148
     creepy crafts and costumes for all ages

6   Quick Tricks   162
     snacks, crafts and decorating on the fly

7   Gooseberry Grab Bag   178
     a treasure trove of stencils and patterns

[*October's poplars are flaming* **torches** *lighting the way to winter.* —NOVA BAIR]

168

52

95

170

84

MISCELLANEOUS

Holiday Planner   198
Resources   201
Our Story   202
Menu Index   203
Project Index   205
Recipe Index   206

pumpkin parade

THE GLOWING FACE of a Jack-o'-Lantern is the mascot of Halloween. Pumpkin designs can be simple or intricate, silly or sinister, abstract or figurative. It all begins with a color, size or shape that stands out at the pumpkin patch or farm stand. Then, the humble squash is transformed into a masterpiece for a fun yet fleeting display!

[*When black cats prowl and pumpkins gleam, may luck be yours on Halloween.*]

—UNKNOWN

pumpkin primer

TIP Inspect your pick for any bruises, cuts or pests that will make it decay quickly. Those with flat bottoms are ideal for sturdy displays, especially when lighting with candles.

ORANGE IS THE COLOR of the classic "Jack," but the heady array of colors, shapes and sizes available at the pumpkin patch has never been more plentiful or fun to experiment with! From the albino Baby Boos and ethereal gray-blues of the Jarrahdales to the downright bizarre textures of the warty alligator-skinned varieties, there's one to suit every fancy. This Halloween let your inner artist shine! Create carved or painted pumpkins that elicit smiles, embellished pumpkins that surprise, or functional pumpkins that light the way, keep drinks cool or simply add a festive touch to your décor.

GROW YOUR OWN. After the last frost of spring, choose a large patch that gets plenty of sunlight and plant seeds of your favorite variety about one-inch deep and at least four feet apart, mulching well. In about three to four months it will be time to select your pick of the patch.

CURE THEM TO LAST. Lightly spray pumpkins with a spray-bottle mixture of 1 quart water and 4 ounces bleach to eliminate surface bacteria. Let the pumpkins cure and harden in a cool, dry place and they might just last an entire season.

Carve individual letters into pumpkins to spell a message or welcome guests to their destination.

pumpkins
carved

ORIGINAL EUROPEAN "Jack's Lanterns" were carved from root vegetables like potatoes, rutabagas, beets or turnips and illuminated by igniting lumps of coal inside. The pilgrims found American pumpkin varieties better suited for carving into Jack-o'-Lanterns.

TIP After carving your pumpkin, smooth a thin film of petroleum jelly over the cut edges to protect it from the damaging effects of air and sunlight.

MAP OUT THE DESIGN you want to carve on paper first. Choose from the stencils in the Gooseberry Grab Bag (page 178), search for clip art online or draw a freehand design.
- Cut out the top of the pumpkin with a very sharp knife, then thoroughly scrape out the flesh and seeds with a fleshing tool, metal spoon or ice cream scoop. Rummage through your kitchen or garage for great carving utensils. See just a few of the many tools you can use on the opposite page.
- Enlarge or reduce your design to fit. Attach it with tape or thumbtacks, then trace it onto the pumpkin by following the outline of the design

with tiny punctures made with a trussing or embroidery needle or another thumbtack.
- Carve along the transferred design with a craft knife, pumpkin-carving tool or paring knife. For etched designs or reliefs, use wood carvers or linoleum cutters. Short blades provide the most control. For a completely different look, drill holes of varying diameter to make patterns. A 5/16-inch drill bit makes holes that are the perfect size for inserting the bulbs of string lights.
- Illuminate your work of art with tealights, string lights or battery-powered votives, depending on how it's arranged in your décor.

Owloween is lots of fun. "Who" says standard Jack-o'-Lantern faces must reign? Leaves, messages and critter designs barely nick the surface of the clever ways to carve a pumpkin.

TOOLS

The pumpkin sculptor's tools are endless. Borrow melon ballers or ice cream scoops, knives and ice picks from the kitchen. Scavenge the garage for saws, drills or routing tools for detail work. Visit craft stores to find specialty tools like linoleum cutters, leather-work or pottery tools... ideal for scraping away a minimum of surface area.

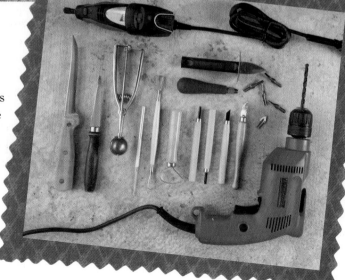

A precious jewel carved most curiously; it is a little picture painted well.
—RICHARD WATSON GILDER

THE KEY TO CARVING success is choosing the right tool for the job. For designs like these that just scrape the surface, use linoleum cutters, woodworking, leatherworking or pottery tools.

All aglow, a pumpkin's daytime grin becomes more mysterious after dark, and a cat's silhouette pops to life when backlit. Look to cookie cutter shapes for a unique spin on the usual faces.

A free-form twist on the usual pumpkin face brings this Jack to life (top left). Linoleum cutters allow you to cut away a minimum of the pumpkin's surface for a muted glow. Carve away the flesh entirely to boldly backlight your design (top right). Use cookie cutters to get the shape you want in a snap. Lightly hammer a metal cutter into the surface of the pumpkin for a perfect cutout with clean edges (above).

painted pumpkins

FOR DECORATED PUMPKINS that last all season, paint is ideal. Paint house numbers, monograms or a series of individual letters on smaller pumpkins to create messages like "BEWARE!" Add elegant shimmer to your outdoor displays by using metallic paints in copper, champagne, gold or bronze. Update the look to last right through the holidays. Simply change out fall's leaves for evergreen boughs and go from autumnal-hued paints to red on white.

WHEN PAINTING PUMPKINS, it's best to start with a cured pumpkin (see page 11), but a clean surface that is thoroughly dry is a must for best adhesion. Mask the stems off with painter's tape, if you wish.

Let your creative side come to life. Choose a palette and repeat it for striking impact.

Stripes on a pumpkin are a cheater's dream. Simply follow the natural ridges of the squash for foolproof artistry.

Monograms are a fun way to personalize your porch or entryway. Paint on house numbers to make finding your home a cinch for guests.

TOOLS

A pumpkin painter's toolbox should contain spray paint in different finishes, spray glitter, gold or silver leaf, metallic acrylic paints, a variety of paint brushes, spray adhesive and painter's tape for masking off areas you want to keep natural.

Ask not what your pumpkin can do for you;
ask what you can do for your pumpkin.

—UNKNOWN

GRAPHIC BLACK-ON-WHITE
is attention-getting and casts an
otherworldly glow outdoors on moonlit
nights. Download stencils from the
Web or choose your favorite from
our Gooseberry Grab Bag
(page 178).

BEYOND THE STANDARD PUMPKIN sphere, look to gourds and winter squash for interesting shapes to conjure up unusual ideas for your designs. Consider rendering white designs on black-painted pumpkins for a more dark and devious spin.

The pear-shaped butternut squash suggests an array of fun uses, from frightening faces like the one shown on the opposite page to bowling pins or point pegs for a ring toss. Simply paint on stripes or numbers, then cut off a small slice from the bottom of each so that they stand upright in formation.

Spiderwebs are easy to render. Start with a center dot, then create "spokes" the length you desire. Connect the spokes with small curved lines to represent the draped silk of the spider's trap.

embellished pumpkins

BUTTONS, RIBBONS, FELT, seeds, pasta and even candy…take a glance at the contents of your sewing box or pantry and create the most remarkable pumpkins on the block! Turn to your glue gun, straight pins or toothpicks to hold items in place. Decorative fasteners like upholstery tacks and brads can serve a dual purpose of function and form.

WHAT COULD BE MORE FITTING for Halloween than a candy-coated pumpkin? But remember, these hot-glued faces are just for show! Stock up all year on seasonal candy so that you have pastel, bright and muted tones for weaving into your designs.

TOOLS
Look everywhere for embellishments for your pumpkin. A glue gun is ideal for holding felt and candy items in place. Pins and tacks secure buttons. Pipe cleaners can be shaped for antennae, hair, eyelashes or jewelry.

[*And one of green, with buttons of sheen…*
Buttons and bands of gold, I mean.
—WILLIAM BRIGHTY RANDS]

WOOL, FELT, RICKRACK, RIBBON...if you would use it to accent a garment, pillow, ponytail (or just about anything) it's perfectly suited for pumpkin styling!

Dare your guests not to smile when they see this fantastically finished trio. A spiky, lit-candle hairdo is unexpected and a unique way to celebrate a birthday. Fill the inside of the pumpkins with bags of candy.

THUMBTACKS, PUSHPINS and upholstery tack studs add bling to these sophisticated spheres. Find them in multiple finishes…bronze, silver, copper, brass or even painted, clear or patterned styles.

party pumpkins

THE MANY SHAPES AND SIZES of pumpkins and gourds lend themselves to an array of uses. A crookneck gourd or butternut squash can be turned into a whimsical finial for stair railings or curtain rods. Hollowed-out pumpkins can be used as dishes for food, loaded with ice and drinks or filled with birdseed and hung from a tree. You are only limited by your creativity. And when the season has passed, perhaps the best function of all is when you layer the remnants in your compost pile to create fertile soil for next spring's pumpkin patch.

Mini pumpkins make lovely votives. Use around metal cookie cutter to remove a circle of flesh from the stem end. Insert a votive or tealight and set it aglow!

A stack of white spray-painted pumpkins capped with a medley of mosses serves as a ghostly topiary on a sideboard.

BRING PUMPKINS INSIDE and put them to use in novel ways. From soup tureens and candleholders to a cooler for iced drinks, pumpkins of all sizes can be impressive forms with function.

A thick-skinned field pumpkin is the perfect vase for this lush centerpiece. Hollow out the pumpkin and insert a water-filled vase of flowers. Don't fill the pumpkin shell with water or you might have a dinnertime flood!

TOOLS

A spray bottle filled with a mild bleach solution is a must for preparing pumpkins for long-term display. Rub all cut surfaces with petroleum jelly to seal out air. Wire comes in handy for securing your creations to wreath forms, fence posts and other displays. Choose candles, battery-powered votives or string lights for illumination.

[*The true function . . . of all art is not to teach, but to interpret life beautifully.*

—CARLETON NOYES]

Set a large hollowed-out pumpkin on a tray to catch leaks and any condensation that forms. Fill it with ice and beverages so thirsty guests can help themselves.

OUTDOORS, let pops of pumpkin-orange light the way, brighten potted arrangements or accent architecture like gateposts, stairs, and windowsills.

Tiny pumpkins are difficult to carve freehand. Mini cookie or aspic cutters do a much better job of this task. Hammer them in lightly and then push them through with the cutout intact (left and below left).

A pitchfork pierces a trio of pumpkin votives to light the way to the front door. Be sure to use battery-powered votives if the display will be left unattended (below).

devilish décor

GHASTLY, HAUNTING, or just plain fun, decorating for Halloween can go in many spirited directions. From colorful porch décor to wall-to-wall wickedness, let the following pages inspire you. Use Mother Nature's castoffs in shades of the sunset to add pops of color to wreaths and centerpieces.

[*Jack-O'-Lanterns grinning, Shadows on a screen,*
Shrieks and starts and laughter...This is Halloween!]

—DOROTHY BROWN THOMPSON

WARY WELCOME

Ghoulish greetings start at the
front door. When a cheery "boo"
won't do, string dark corners with
spiderwebs and a critter or two!
A blood-red velvet drape tied
back with a noose offers a
glimpse of a chalked message
sure to give guests pause.

Bundles of dried corn husks add drama
to this entry. Add pumpkins and Indian
corn for a harvest theme, or go gothic
with pewter accents like this candelabra
and dark raven poised for flight. Artificial
birds can be found at craft stores and are
easily attached to displays with
floral wire.

Turn a side table into a serving station with the addition of a tarnished silver tray set with goblets brimming with simply refreshing...or downright spine-tingling...potions.

An ominous vulture looks ready to swoop in for the leftovers. This eerie little birdie adds to the oddity of this Old World spin on Halloween décor.

GREET YOUR GUESTS in the foyer with a tasty sipper (top) and a decorative display that seems out of another time: blind-folded portraits, prehistoric-size bugs in shadow box frames and a dried bouquet from a forgotten special occasion (left).

SINISTER SIDEBOARD

When it's a more haunting look you're after, add some spooky touches to everyday accessories for frightful delight. It's simple to build a haunted scene with inexpensive props and items you may already have. Glass canisters from the kitchen and bath become creepy specimen jars.

SET A HAUNTED TABLE

For an American Gothic dining room, use contrasting elements like black and white, rough surfaces and delicate textures and a mix of silver and brass.

MENU

APPETIZERS:
Severed Head Cheese
Eye Eye Balls
Poison Apples

COCKTAIL:
Eternal Damnation

DESSERT:
Beastly Bat Treats
Death By Chocolate

ON TOP OF AN ANTIQUE oval mirror, pedestals are fashioned out of industrial spools trimmed in black lace. Lengths of lace and strands of crystals transform a traditional chandelier into an eerie corona. Other dark dressings might include ribbon-tied surgical instruments, plastic bones, small bottles labeled "poison" or mousetraps with plastic "caught" mice.

Let them die a happy death by chocolate with blocks upon blocks of chocolate set on a black-lace-trimmed pedestal with a cleaver for chopping...if you dare!

Set the table with beautiful china and silver in dark motifs and dramatic shapes. Add "garnishes" like bugs and leaves for a bit of festive drama.

EMBELLISH YOUR DOOR
with a bucket of blooms and a tangled grapevine arch for a happy Halloween effect. Choose flowers in shades of the season and group them for impact.

Autumn is a second spring when every leaf is a flower

—ALBERT CAMUS

WINDOWBOX WHIMSY

Decked out for the season in combustible colors, this full-sun windowbox celebrates everything we love about fall… like the vivid colors and leafy textures. All the plants and supplies are readily available at your home-improvement store's garden center or nursery.

MATERIALS:

purple fountain grass
variegated Japanese sedge
florist mums
small white pumpkins
ornamental peppers

Gleaming white "Lumina" (large) and "Snowball" (small) pumpkins mixed with shiny tufts of black-as-night mondo grass make a simple full-shade combination that's all-hallows spooky but oh-so neat. Bursting clusters of blood-orange berries drip from branches of bittersweet vine (sold in bunches at florist shops). You can boost the ghostly glow by hiding strands of mini lights between the pumpkins.

MATERIALS:

black mondo grass
small white pumpkins
large white pumpkins
bittersweet (cut branches)

MATERIALS:

wooden planter box
plastic foam blocks
glue
sheet moss
black paper
mini pumpkins
backyard branches and twigs
craft wire
corrugated craft cardboard

WINDOW WHIMSY

• **Paint** and embellish a wooden planter as desired and let dry.
• **Trim** to fit, then glue plastic foam blocks in the planter and cover with sheet moss.
• **Cut** a face from black paper and glue onto a miniature pumpkin.
• **Glue** the pumpkin to a twig. Tightly twist a long length of craft wire around the stem, pumpkin and stick several times to secure the pumpkin to the stick. Curl the wire ends. "Plant" the pumpkin in the box.
• **Fill** in and around the pumpkins with more sticks and twigs. Cut "leaves" from corrugated cardboard and glue randomly to the twigs.

HOMESPUN HALLOWEEN

Create a creepy vignette on the front hall table. A simple arrangement of everyday items…lanterns, pillows, candlesticks mixed with pumpkins and a watchful owl become eerie with the addition of a tangle of webs and the flicker of candlelight.

WELCOMING "BOO!"

- **Use** a copy machine to enlarge the patterns on page 187 to fit a sisal mat...this one came with a black fabric binding.
- **Cut** out the letters and arrange them on the mat. Use a marker to lightly trace around each letter; repeat for the candy corn pattern.
- **Paint** the designs. After the paint is good and dry, use a black paint pen to outline the candy corn sections.
- **Finish** off with a strip of green grosgrain ribbon glued along the inside edges of the binding.

MATERIALS:

craft sticks
2½- and 4-inch foam balls
craft glue
black tissue paper
black acrylic paint
bumpy pipe cleaners
large-head straight pins
small white beads

CREEPY CRAWLERS

- **Use** a craft stick to connect two foam balls for the body. Cover with craft glue and small pieces of tissue paper. Once dry, paint it black.
- **Cut** four bumpy pipe cleaners in half for legs; insert four legs into each side of the body.
- **Thread** 1 bead for each eye onto a large-head straight pin and press into the spider.

PUMPKIN TOWERS

Height makes an impact and few things are easier than stacking plump pumpkins for an impressive display. Indoors or out, these designs are easy autumn versions of winter's jolly, happy soul…minus the corncob pipe…which you can always add, if you'd like!

Take the pumpkin stack concept to the highest heights by making this statement at your garden entry or front gate.

MATERIALS:

3 pumpkins (in graduated sizes)
small block of wood (piece of 4x4 works great)
2½-foot metal rebar
bowl-shaped terra cotta pot
bag of concrete
pine cones
bittersweet vine

• **Drill** a pilot hole in the wood smaller than the diameter of the rebar. Tap the rebar into the hole with a hammer until secure. Center the wood block with rebar in the terra cotta bowl.
• **Pour** dry cement around the wooden block three to four inches deep for a base. Fill the bowl with water and let the concrete set for twenty-four hours.
• **Select** three pumpkins in graduated sizes. Drill small holes in the bottoms and tops of the two biggest pumpkins and slide them onto the rebar so the largest rests on bottom. Drill a small hole in the bottom of the smallest pumpkin to cap the arrangement. Use pine cones as spacers if the rebar is longer than the span of the pumpkins. Hide the base with leaves and add a garland of bittersweet vine.

MATERIALS:
1 wide planter
2 pumpkins (in graduated sizes)
bag of Spanish moss
wooden dowel
Styrofoam or florist foam
   (optional)
paring knife or drill

• **Choose** pumpkins in a mix of shades or a single hue. Select a container wide enough for the largest pumpkin to rest in. A block of foam can be placed inside the container to stabilize the bottom pumpkin.

• **Measure** and cut a wooden dowel long enough to connect the pumpkins.

• **Cut** out the stem of the larger pumpkin with a sharp knife and insert the dowel. With a paring knife or drill, cut a small hole in the bottom of the smaller pumpkin and set it on top of the larger pumpkin (fitting the dowel in the hole). Fill in the gaps between the pumpkins with moss.

GRINNING GOURDS

If you dislike seeing your carved pumpkin handiwork cave in over time, consider carving hard-shell gourds instead. This indoor collection of ghoulish grins won't invite pests...only smiles! They can be stored after Halloween in a cool, dry place and used season after season. Gourds make great birdhouses, too!

MATERIALS:

3 medium-size dried gourds
hobby rotary tool and 1/8-inch router
  bit or cutter (or electric drill, 1-inch
  hold saw and mini hacksaw)
pencil
scissors
yellow tissue paper
masking tape
1 strand (35) white twinkle lights

• **Cut** a large hole in the bottom of a gourd using the rotary tool and ⅛-inch bit. (If using an electric drill bit and hole saw, cut a hole and enlarge it with the mini hacksaw.) Clean out seeds and debris.

• **Use** a pencil to lightly sketch a face onto the gourd. A simple design works best. Secure the gourd between two stationary objects and cut out the face with the rotary tool (or electric drill and mini hacksaw). Take your time...it's easy to accidentally crack the brittle gourd.

• **Cut** a large tissue-paper square to fit behind the face. Tape paper in place inside the gourd. Repeat the process with the remaining gourds. Arrange the trio in a large shallow bowl or container. Tuck a portion of the white lights inside each gourd, with the plug extended over the container's edge.

• **Add** miniature Indian corn and small fresh gourds as a finishing touch for the arrangement. Sunflowers and autumn leaves work well, too, for concealing the cord.

JUICE-O'-LANTERN

Decorating oranges usually means making aromatic, clove-studded pomanders for the holidays, but this sunny citrus is the perfect color and shape for fashioning into miniature "Jacks" for Halloween.

MATERIALS:

oranges
plastic top from spice jar
pen or felt-tip marker
knife
melon baller
spoon
craft knife
tealight candles
florist clay

• **Draw** a circle around the top of an orange using the top of a spice jar as a template. Then draw a face onto the side of the orange. (A pen or felt-tip marker works best.) Slice off the top of the orange, using the circle you drew as a guide. Scoop out the contents with a melon baller, using a knife to cut the fruit away from the sides of the orange.

• **Place** the curve of a large spoon inside the orange, against the drawn face. Using a craft knife, cut out the features of the Jack-o'-Lantern. (The spoon provides a surface to press against and protects your fingers from the knife.)

• **Set** a tealight candle inside the orange. Arrange the Jack-o'-Lanterns on a mantel or table in combination with leaves and berries. Use a small piece of florist clay to keep each candleholder attached to your display.

MUM'S THE WORD

In September chrysanthemums appear in grocery stores, flower markets and at the pumpkin patch in shades that match the flaming foliage of maples and oaks. Use these inexpensive, lasting blooms in multiple ways in your décor.

Simple floral wreaths brighten front doors and offer a warm welcome! A tapestry of fall hues is woven together here by first repeating flowers like the brown-eyed "Viking" mums around the form to establish a color pattern then filling in with blooms in complementary shades.

• **Soak** a florist foam wreath form thoroughly in a mixture of water and flower food diluted according to the label instructions. Reinforce the form by repeatedly wrapping a piece of florist tape around one area; then fasten a piece of wire over it to make a hanger. Position the wire loop at the form's plastic back for easy hanging (below).

• **Cut** each flower just below the bloom head, leaving a stem about one inch long. Push stems into the foam so that the blossoms hug the surface. Fill the form completely, grouping similar colors (below right).

SUNNY SPHERES

Give chrysanthemums a new look in an unexpected way. Brilliant green, button-type "Kermit" mum spheres add a striking accent to vases, centerpieces…even window ledges. The arrangements here and on the previous page will last a week or longer if the foam is kept moist. Water every two days by placing them in the kitchen sink and spraying gently to moisten the foam. Allow excess water to drain completely.

Many grocery stores have floral departments that are good sources for basic flower supplies. Florist foam balls come in an assortment of sizes. The ones shown here are 2-inch spheres that, when covered with flowers, appear almost twice that size (below left).

• **Soak** the foam balls in water and flower food diluted to label instructions.
• **Cut** the flower stems about an inch under the bloom head.
• **Push** stems into the forms, with flowers touching or overlapping. Add flowers until the sphere is covered.

MATERIALS

assorted mums
florist foam wreath or spheres
flower food
florist tape
wire
scissors

Serving pieces have a multitude of uses. What organizes silverware or condiments on the table becomes a candy caddy and lip-smacking arrangement when put to novel use at Halloween.

Celebrate

TOPIARY MAGIC
In-season citrus brightens the base of this simple topiary. Bundle a dozen orange carnations into a tight bouquet then insert them into a cube of soaked florist foam set into a ceramic mixing bowl. The citrus hides the foam, but you can "mulch" with any number of goodies…Halloween candy, acorns or mini pumpkins.

IT'S A WRAP

Quickly customize a vase of flowers. Place a vase in the center of a sheet of wrapping paper that complements the colors of your bouquet. Gather the paper in folds around the neck of the vase, and tie the paper in place with strands of raffia or a piece of ribbon. Add water and flowers. Now that's magic!

EASY AS PIE

Tiny pastry tins filled with water make whimsical containers for individual flower heads. Place the tins on a tray or platter, and then add the blooms. Use different sizes of tins and flowers for a pretty arrangement.

CHAPTER 3

Halloween Open House
Spooktacular Block Party
Bewitching "Boo"ffet
Masquerade Party
Pumpkin Patch Picnic
Fright Night Film Festival
Creepy Cookie Swap
Cauldronluck
Scary School Party
Never-Slumber Party

ghoulish
gatherings

SUMMON YOUR BEST GHOULS and goblins
for some fun this Halloween! Whether it's a
masked adult soirée with delicious nibbles
disguised as creepy-crawlies or block-party
fun fit for the entire neighborhood, we've
come up with an assortment of eerie and
inspired party themes sure to give you
goosebumps.

Eat, drink and be scary. —UNKNOWN

entertaining tips

NEVER FEAR

Anybody can host a gathering indoors or out, whether cozy home or stately mansion. The only magic involved is a bit of advanced planning…and a sense of humor.

SCARE UP SOME FUN

If you want to throw a Halloween bash with a harvest feel, incorporate natural elements of the season into your décor at every turn. If it's "creepy" you're after, run with it…critters under cloches, frightening foods, and jaw-dropping centerpieces created from the unexpected: plastic bones, insects and dripping moss. Our Devilish Décor chapter (page 28) will help you go wild!

MASTER YOUR MENU

Our enticing array of entertaining ideas is sure to inspire fun. We've picked recipes that will catch your guests' attention, satisfy their need to nibble and leave you with the reputation of "most spooktacular host" in town. From a Halloween Open House (page 50) replete with make-ahead comfort food to fun ideas for a Scary School Party (page 112) that's sure to get kids in the Halloween spirit, we've left no…tombstone…unturned.

October 31st

Madison Sides

Suzanne James

Pete St. John

Alex Yeast

Patricia Trent

Robert Strange

Katherine Cobbs

BURY EXCUSES

Impromptu parties can be the most fun of all, especially at Halloween. Dead flowers in vases are actually allowed. Got cobwebs? Pretend you planned it! Still worried you can't get it together? Look to our Quick Tricks chapter (page 162) so you can throw a ghostly gathering on a worry-free whim.

Epitaphs

Gone Away Owing More th...
I could Pay

I Went to heaven and back aga...

I told you I was sick.

Pardon me for not risin...

...She kicked up her heels a...
away she went.

...here lies an honest lawyer...
that _is_ strange

I ate your food and then I was bo...

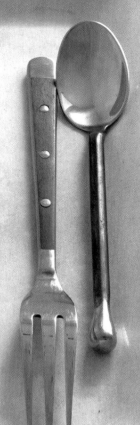

MENU

Brew-Ha-Ha Punch

A Great Pumpkin
Cheese Ball

Maple-Topped Sweet
Potato Skins

Fennel, Apple &
Celery Slaw*

Boil & Bubble Soup
Cauldron

Jack-o'-Lantern Bread

Crustless Pumpkin Pie

*double recipe
Serves 10 to 12

Halloween Open House

OPEN YOUR DOOR and let good spirits in. Autumn nights are ideal for entertaining, and this easy supper is a divine way to revive after a night of trick-or-treating. Kids can sort candy and relive the fun while the adults relax and visit.

Some shining notice will be 'there,' of open house and ready fare.
—WILLIAM WORDSWORTH

Brew-Ha-Ha Punch

An emerald-green elixir is a perfectly creepy libation for Halloween night.

2 c. sugar
2 qts. water
2 (0.13-oz.) envs. lime drink mix
46-oz. can pineapple juice
1 qt. ginger ale

Stir together sugar and 2 quarts water until sugar is dissolved. Stir in remaining ingredients. Chill. Makes 4 quarts.

VARIATION

For the closer-to-the-grave guests who wish to partake in a more potent version of this brew, simply add 10 ounces of white rum to the concoction.

A Great Pumpkin Cheese Ball

Add the stem from a real pumpkin and your guests will do a double take. A broccoli stem is another…edible… option.

8-oz. pkg. cream cheese, softened
10-oz. container sharp Cheddar cold-pack
   cheese spread
¼ c. crumbled blue cheese
2 t. Worcestershire sauce
¼ t. celery salt
¼ t. onion salt
½ c. walnuts, finely chopped
1 t. paprika
Garnishes: 1 pretzel rod, broken in half, and
   assorted crackers

Blend together the cheeses until smooth. Stir in the Worcestershire sauce, celery salt and onion salt, adding more to taste, if desired. Shape into a ball and set on a serving plate; cover and chill 2 to 3 hours or until firm.

   Score cheese ball with vertical lines, if desired, to resemble a pumpkin. Toss walnuts with paprika; press into surface of cheese ball. Break a pretzel rod in half and insert in top for stem, if desired. Arrange crackers around cheese ball. Serves 10 to 12.

Kids will giggle over the floating "hands" in their bewitching brew! Rinse out a pair of vinyl gloves and fill with water. Tie the ends tightly into knots and place in the freezer. When frozen, cut off the knots, remove the gloves and float in punch.

A Great Pumpkin Cheese Ball

Wrap napkins and silverware with bittersweet vines for a natural accent. If the bittersweet won't bend easily, run under warm water and place in a paper bag to soften. Natural raffia or burlap twine lends a more rustic touch.

Maple-Topped Sweet Potato Skins

Sweet potato skins offer a tasty alternative to regular potato skins. These are loaded with spices and topped with sugary walnuts…a savory-sweet side dish for any dinner.

6 sweet potatoes
½ c. cream cheese, softened
¼ c. sour cream
2 t. cinnamon, divided
2 t. nutmeg, divided
2 t. ground ginger, divided
2 c. walnuts or pecans, chopped
¼ c. brown sugar, packed
3 T. butter, softened
Garnishes: maple syrup, apple slices,
  additional nuts

Pierce potatoes with a fork. Place on an ungreased baking sheet. Bake at 400 degrees for 45 minutes to one hour or microwave on high 15 to 20 minutes, or until tender; cool.

Slice each potato in half lengthwise; scoop out pulp, keeping skins intact. Mash pulp in a mixing bowl until smooth; add cream cheese, sour cream and one teaspoon each of spices. Mix well and spoon into potato skins. Stir together nuts, brown sugar, butter and remaining spices; sprinkle over top. Place potato skins on an ungreased baking sheet; bake at 400 degrees for 15 minutes. If desired, drizzle with warm syrup and garnish with apple slices and additional nuts. Serves 12.

VARIATION

For a savory version, mash the pulp with ½ cup grated Parmesan cheese, the finely grated zest and juice of 1 orange, 3 teaspoons salt, 2 teaspoons ground pepper and 3 tablespoons butter; garnish with ⅓ cup lightly toasted pine nuts.

Fennel, Apple & Celery Slaw

Fennel has a delicate licorice flavor and adds a pleasant note in this tangy slaw with apples. This make-ahead side dish is perfect for entertaining and easily doubled for this crowd.

1 T. cider vinegar
1 T. molasses
1 t. Dijon mustard
½ t. salt
¼ t. pepper
¼ c. olive oil
1 fennel bulb, trimmed, cored and cut into very thin strips
2 Granny Smith apples, cut into strips
2 Gala apples, cut into strips
2 ribs celery, thinly sliced

Whisk together first 5 ingredients in a large bowl; slowly pour in oil, whisking constantly.

Add fennel, apple and celery to dressing, tossing to combine. Cover and chill up to 4 hours. Toss well just before serving. Serves 8.

Fennel, Apple & Celery Slaw

Boil & Bubble Soup Cauldron

The hominy can pass for teeth and the green peas as beady little eyes. If making soup ahead, don't add peas; cover soup when cool and chill, then add peas when reheating. For a tureen, use a rustic pan, such as a cast-iron Dutch oven. Or you can use a pumpkin shell. You'll need a pumpkin at least 12 to 16 inches tall and wide. Cut off top and scoop out seeds. About 10 minutes before serving, fill shell with boiling water to warm. Drain and fill with hot soup. Use the top as a lid for the pumpkin tureen.

1 T. oil
2 lbs. uncooked turkey Italian sausages, casings removed
1 onion, chopped
1 red pepper, chopped
2 cloves garlic, pressed or minced
1 T. chili powder
2 t. cumin seed
1 t. dried oregano
2 qts. chicken broth
2 lbs. banana or Hubbard squash, peeled and cut into ½-inch cubes
3 (15-oz.) cans hominy, drained
10-oz. pkg. frozen peas
salt and pepper

Heat oil in an 8- to 10-quart pan over medium-high heat. Add sausages to pan and break into bite-size pieces. Stir occasionally until lightly browned, about 5 minutes.

Add onion, red pepper and garlic; sauté over high heat until onion is soft, about 5 minutes. Stir in chili powder, cumin seed and oregano. Add broth, cover and bring to a boil over high heat.

Add squash to soup. Return to a boil. Reduce heat, cover and simmer until squash is tender when pierced, about 15 minutes, stirring occasionally.

Add hominy and peas, separating if necessary. Bring soup to a boil over high heat and boil about 3 minutes.

Pour soup into a tureen and ladle into mugs or bowls. Add salt and pepper to taste. Serves 10 to 12.

Boil & Bubble
Soup Cauldron

For a seated dinner, instead of using a big hollowed-out pumpkin as a soup tureen, turn smaller sugar pumpkins into individual soup bowls. Hollow out several, fill each with soup and replace the pumpkin "lid" to keep soup warm. Set several on a platter surrounded with real pumpkin leaves and curly vines.

Jack-o'-Lantern Bread

Jack-o'-Lantern Bread

Follow package directions for thawing bread dough. If making ahead, wrap cooled bread airtight and keep at room temperature up to one day or freeze to store longer. Reheat (thaw, if frozen), loosely covered with foil, in a 350-degree oven 10 to 15 minutes, or until warm.

2 (1-lb.) loaves frozen bread dough, thawed
1 T. beaten egg
1½ t. milk

Place the loaves in a bowl. Cover bowl with plastic wrap and let rise until doubled, 45 minutes to one hour.

Punch dough down, knead loaves together in bowl and shape into a ball.

Transfer ball to a greased 15"x12" baking sheet. With greased hands or a lightly floured rolling pin, flatten ball into a 13"x11" oval. Cut out eyes, nose, and mouth; openings should be at least 1½ to 2 inches wide. (To make small loaves, divide dough into 4 equal pieces and roll into 6"x4" ovals; eye, nose and mouth openings should be at least 1 to 1 ½ inches wide.) Lift out cut-out dough and bake on another pan or use for decoration.

Cover the shaped dough lightly with plastic wrap and let rise until puffy, about 20 minutes.

Mix egg with milk; brush over dough.

Bake at 350 degrees for 30 to 35 minutes or until golden. Cool on a wire rack. Serve warm or cool. Serves 10 to 12.

Crustless Pumpkin Pie

Deliciously different!

4 eggs, beaten
15-oz. can pumpkin
12-oz. can evaporated milk
1 ½ c. sugar
2 t. pumpkin pie spice
1 t. salt
18 ¼-oz. pkg. yellow cake mix
1 c. chopped pecans
1 c. butter, melted
Optional: whipped topping, chopped walnuts, cinnamon or nutmeg

Be sure to set a treat table at your Halloween get-together. Fill vintage-style painted metal pails with cello bags of cookies and candies. For a fun twist, cinch each bag closed with a black licorice whip.

Crustless
Pumpkin Pie

Combine eggs, pumpkin, evaporated milk, sugar, spice and salt. Mix well and pour into an ungreased 13"x9" baking pan. Sprinkle dry cake mix and nuts over top. Drizzle with butter; do not stir.

Bake at 350 degrees for 45 minutes to one hour, or until a toothpick inserted in center comes out clean. Serve with whipped topping sprinkled with nuts and cinnamon or nutmeg, if desired. Serves 8 to 10.

VARIATION

Whipped cream is a wonderful addition to warm desserts. In a chilled bowl, use an electric mixer to beat 2 cups heavy whipping cream, gradually adding ¼ cup sugar and beating until stiff. Make it even more special by adding 2 drops of pumpkin or hazelnut flavoring, or a dash of espresso powder.

MENU

Hot Mulled Cider

Scarlet Sangria*

Monsteroni Salad

Goblin Dip &
Bone Crackers

Mummy Hot Dogs

Don't-Be-A-Chicken
Chili*

Pumpkin Ice Cream

Tangled Web Rice Pops

*double recipe

Serves 10 to 12

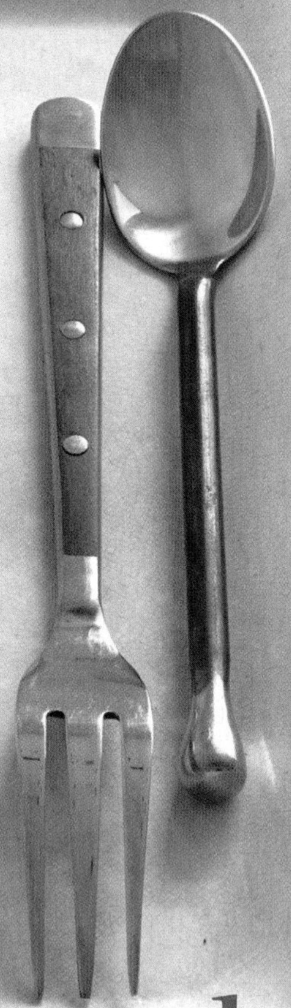

Spooktacular Block Party

ORGANIZE A BLOCK PARTY early
in the evening on Halloween
night so bellies can be full of
food before the candy eating
commences. Hold a costume
contest and give out ribbons
for scariest, silliest, best in show
and most creative.

*When men were **scary** of witch and fairy, of haunted castle, of spook and elf...*
—EDWIN MEADE ROBINSON

Hot Mulled Cider

Hot Mulled Cider

Float a few apple slices and some cinnamon sticks in this warming drink.

2 qts. apple cider
1 orange, quartered
¼ c. brown sugar, packed
¼ t. pumpkin pie spice
2 (4-inch) cinnamon sticks
6 whole cloves

Combine all ingredients in a 3-quart slow cooker; cover and cook on low setting 2 to 4 hours. Remove orange sections and spices before serving. Serves 10 to 12.

VARIATION

For a different twist, combine one quart apple cider with one quart apricot nectar and add some slices of fresh ginger root to the mix.

Scarlet Sangria

Grown-ups will appreciate this fruited-wine cocktail. Double or triple this recipe for a big gathering. It can be served warm, too (see Variation).

1 navel orange, halved
1 lime, halved
Optional: 1⅓ c. merlot, chilled
1⅓ c. pomegranate juice, chilled
¼ c. sugar
8.4-oz. bottle sparkling apple cider, chilled

Squeeze 2 tablespoons juice from one orange half; squeeze one tablespoon juice from one lime half. Cut remaining orange and lime halves into thin slices.

Combine citrus juices, wine, pomegranate juice and sugar in a pitcher, stirring until sugar dissolves. Slowly add sparkling cider, stirring gently. Add citrus slices; serve immediately. Serves 4.

VARIATION

To make warm sangria, substitute regular apple cider for the sparkling variety and warm gently in a slow cooker or over a low flame on your stovetop. Serve in coffee mugs or to-go cups.

Monsteroni Salad

1½ c. elbow macaroni, cooked
3 c. sliced mushrooms, diced
15 cherry tomatoes, halved
1 c. yellow or red pepper, sliced
½ c. green onions, chopped
¾ c. sliced black olives, drained
1 c. crumbled feta cheese
Optional: ¾ c. pepperoni, diced
½ c. olive oil
½ c. red wine vinegar
1½ t. garlic powder
1½ t. dried basil
1½ t. dried oregano
¾ t. pepper
¾ t. sugar

In a large bowl, combine macaroni, vegetables, cheese and pepperoni, if desired; set aside. Whisk together remaining ingredients in a small bowl. Pour over macaroni mixture and toss until evenly coated. Cover and chill 2 hours to overnight. Serves 10 to 12.

Goblin Dip & Bone Crackers

16-oz. can chili without beans
16-oz. can refried beans
8-oz. pkg. cream cheese
8-oz. jar chunky pico de gallo
4½-oz. can chopped green chiles
½ t. ground cumin
Toppings: Cheddar or Monterey Jack cheese
    with peppers, chopped black olives, sliced
    green onions
Bone Crackers (See Note)

Combine first 6 ingredients in a heavy saucepan over low heat, stirring often, for 15 minutes, or until cheese is melted. Transfer to a bowl, sprinkle with desired toppings and serve warm with Bone Crackers. Makes 6 cups.

NOTE
Cut flour tortillas with a bone-shaped cookie cutter. Spray "bones" lightly with cooking spray and bake at 350° for 10 minutes.

Goblin Dip & Bone
Crackers

Mummy
Hot Dogs

Before dark falls and trick-or-treating commences, keep the kids occupied bobbing for apples or playing games like Red Rover, 3-legged races and doughnut-eating contests.

Mummy Hot Dogs

Hot dogs with a Halloween twist!

11-oz. tube refrigerated bread stick dough
12 hot dogs
1 egg
1 T. water
Garnish: mustard

Separate dough into strips. Wrap one strip of dough around each hot dog, leaving ½ inch uncovered for face. Arrange on a lightly greased baking sheet.

Whisk together egg and water; brush over dough. Bake at 350 degrees for 14 to 16 minutes, or until golden. Dot mustard on hot dogs with a toothpick to form eyes, if desired. Serves 12.

Don't-Be-A-Chicken Chili

Sour cream and whipping cream are stirred into this chili, making it extra rich and creamy. Double this recipe and keep it warm for your guests in a 5-quart slow cooker.

1 T. oil
1 lb. boneless, skinless chicken breasts, cubed
1 onion, chopped
14-oz. can chicken broth
2 (15.8-oz.) cans Great Northern beans, drained and rinsed
2 (4 ½-oz.) cans chopped green chiles
1½ t. garlic powder
1 t. salt
1 t. ground cumin
½ t. dried oregano
8-oz. container sour cream
1 c. whipping cream
2 c. shredded Monterey Jack cheese
Garnish: cilantro sprigs

Heat oil in a large skillet over medium heat; add chicken and onion. Sauté 10 minutes, or until chicken is cooked through; set aside.

Combine broth, beans, undrained chiles and seasonings in a large Dutch oven. Bring to a boil over medium-high heat. Add chicken mixture; reduce heat and simmer 30 minutes. Add sour cream and whipping cream, stirring well. Top each serving with shredded cheese; garnish, if desired. Serves 6 to 8.

Don't-Be-A-Chicken Chili

[*The true essentials of a feast are only fun and feed.*]
—HOLMES

Pumpkin Ice Cream

Pumpkin Ice Cream

As yummy as pumpkin pie...without the crust! Freeze in a 13"x9" pan, and use Halloween cookie cutters to make individual servings.

½ gal. vanilla ice cream, softened
1 c. canned pumpkin
½ c. brown sugar, packed
½ t. ground ginger
¼ t. cinnamon
¼ t. nutmeg
1 T. orange juice

Place ice cream in a large bowl; set aside. Mix remaining ingredients with an electric mixer on low speed; blend into ice cream. Cover and freeze. Let soften slightly before scooping for serving. Serves 8 to 10.

To give favorite recipes a Halloween spin...dress them up in new ways. Add warm autumnal spices like cinnamon and nutmeg or pumpkin pie spice to desserts or warm beverages. Blend canned pumpkin into milkshakes and quickbreads.

Tangled Web Rice Pops

Tangled Web Rice Pops

For a guaranteed hit, garnish these yummy treats with bug candies or sprinkles in Halloween shapes and colors.

3 T. butter
10-oz. pkg. marshmallows
6 to 7 c. crispy rice cereal
12 popsicle sticks
6-oz. pkg. semi-sweet chocolate chips, melted
½ c. white chocolate chips, melted
Optional: mini semi-sweet chocolate chips

Melt butter in a large saucepan over low heat. Add marshmallows; cook and stir until melted. Remove from heat; stir in cereal until well coated. Press evenly into a lightly greased 13"x9" baking pan. Cool slightly; cut into 12 bars. Insert a stick in each; set on wax paper to cool. Dip in melted chocolate to coat; let cool slightly and drizzle with melted white chocolate. Immediately sprinkle with mini chips, if desired. Makes one dozen.

TIP
Melt chocolate chips in a double boiler over hot water, or in a microwave-safe bowl (microwave on high one minute, stir and microwave an additional 15 seconds as needed). Stir until smooth.

MENU

Dressed-Up Caramel Apples
(page 145)

Bite-You-Back Pecans

Blood Orange Martinis

Caramelized Onion Dip

Field Salad with Pears &
Blue Cheese*

Roast Pork with Sage &
Pecan Pesto

Sweet Potato Galette

Green Beans Almondine

Ginger Streusel-Topped
Cheesecake

*double recipe
Serves 6 to 8

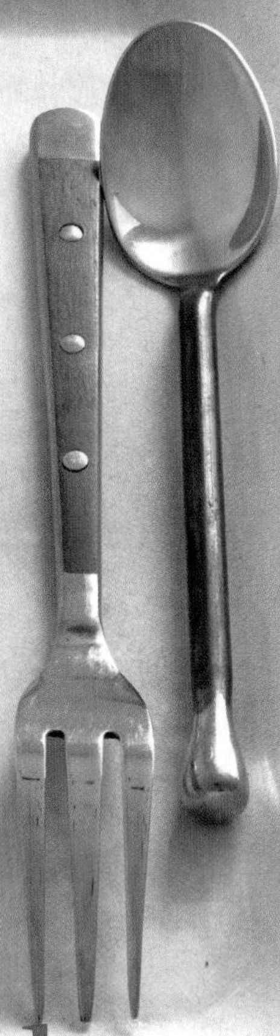

Bite-You-Back Pecans,
page 68

Bewitching "Boo"ffet

WHEN THE CHILL of October
has begun to set in, invite
friends over for an elegant
night in. Set the sideboard with
candles and varied delights…
and don't forget to dim the
lights. Some eerie music might
just fit the bill, or spooky haunted
house sounds if you want
added thrill.

Dressed-Up Caramel Apples,
page 145

October gave a party; The leaves by hundreds came . . . The chestnuts, oaks, and maples, and leaves of every name.
—GEORGE COOPER

Bite-You-Back Pecans

Eat one and you'll soon find yourself drawn back for more. These spicy nuts are addictive.

16-oz. pkg. pecan halves
¼ c. butter, melted
1 T. chili powder
1 t. dried basil
1 t. dried oregano
1 t. dried thyme
1 t. salt
½ t. onion powder
¼ t. garlic powder
¼ t. cayenne pepper

Combine all ingredients in a 2-quart slow cooker. Cover and cook on high setting 15 minutes. Turn to low setting and cook, uncovered, 2 hours, stirring occasionally. Transfer nuts to a baking sheet; cool completely. Store in an airtight container. Makes 4½ cups.

VARIATION

For a smoky flavor, substitute one tablespoon Spanish smoked paprika for the chili powder in this recipe.

~~~~~~~~~~~~

Blood Orange Martinis

Serve this ruby sipper in miniature, sugar-rimmed martini glasses....try orange and yellow sugar sprinkles for a festive flair!

4 c. blood orange juice
2 c. orange-flavored vodka or sparkling water
1 c. orange liqueur or orange juice
Garnish: blood orange slices
Optional: black sanding sugar

In a large pitcher, combine first 3 ingredients and Simple Syrup. Cover and chill until ready to serve. Garnish, if desired. Serve in sugar-rimmed glasses, if desired (see Note). Makes about 8 cups.

NOTE

For sugared rims, dip rims of stemmed glasses into a thin coating of light corn syrup or water, then spin rims in a plateful of sanding sugar.

Blood Orange Martinis

Tie a tag to the stem of each guest's glass (like these ghoulish toe tags with each guest's stats) as a humorous way to identify poured drinks.

Simple Syrup:

½ c. sugar
½ c. water

Bring the sugar and water to a boil in a saucepan. Boil, stirring often, 3 minutes or until sugar dissolves and syrup is reduced to ⅔ cup. Remove from heat; cool completely. Store in refrigerator. Makes ⅔ cup.

Caramelized Onion Dip

Here's a new take on a classic appetizer. Look for sturdy sweet potato chips for scooping up this mega-cheesy family favorite.

2 T. butter
3 onions, thinly sliced
8-oz. pkg. cream cheese, softened
8-oz. pkg. Swiss cheese, shredded
1 c. grated Parmesan cheese
1 c. mayonnaise
sweet potato chips

Melt butter in a large skillet over medium heat; add sliced onions. Cook, stirring often, 30 to 40 minutes, or until onions are caramel colored.

Combine onions, cream cheese, and next 3 ingredients, stirring well. Spoon dip into a lightly greased 1½- to 2-quart casserole dish. Bake, uncovered, at 375 degrees for 30 minutes, or until golden and bubbly. Serve with sweet potato chips. Makes 4 cups.

NOTE
Dip can be prepared a day ahead, but do not bake. Cover and refrigerate overnight. Bake, uncovered, at 375 degrees for 45 minutes, or until golden and bubbly.

Caramelized Onion Dip

Field Salad with Pears
& Blue Cheese

Field Salad with Pears & Blue Cheese

Offer this colorful salad during the fall and winter when pears are in season and fresh walnuts are abundant. For this get together, double the recipe.

5-oz. pkg. salad greens
1 red pear, thinly sliced
¼ c. crumbled blue cheese
3 T. raspberry vinaigrette salad dressing
2 T. walnuts, finely chopped

Combine first 3 ingredients in a large bowl. Add dressing and toss gently. Spoon onto plates and sprinkle evenly with walnuts. Serves 4.

VARIATION
For a fun Halloween embellishment, add "Dracula's Teeth" to this salad by garnishing plated salads with a sprinkling of pomegranate seeds.

Roast Pork with Sage & Pecan Pesto

Be careful not to overprocess the flavorful herb pesto for this dish. The finished sauce should have some texture remaining.

2 qts. apple cider
¼ c. kosher salt
½ c. plus 3 T. fresh sage, chopped and divided
4-lb. boneless pork loin roast
1 t. pepper
2 T. olive oil
Garnish: fresh sage, unshelled pecans

Combine cider, salt and ½ cup sage, stirring until salt dissolves. Place pork in plastic zipping bag; add cider mixture. Seal bag; chill 12 to 24 hours.

Remove pork from brine and pat dry with paper towels. Sprinkle pork with pepper. Heat oil in a large skillet over medium-high heat; add pork.

Cook 6 minutes, or until browned on all sides, turning pork occasionally. Place pork on a rack in a lightly greased roasting pan. Sprinkle remaining 3 tablespoons sage over pork.

Bake, uncovered, at 350 degrees for one hour to one hour and 25 minutes, or until a meat thermometer inserted into thickest part of roast registers 150 degrees. Remove from oven; cover and let rest 10 minutes or until thermometer reaches 160 degrees before slicing. Garnish platter, if desired. Serve with Sage & Pecan Pesto. Serves 8.

Instead of a menu board or cards, use inexpensive slate tiles as trivets for the dishes on your sideboard. Stick adhesive felt dots on the bottom of each to protect your furniture. Write the name of each dish in chalk directly on the tiles.

Sage & Pecan Pesto:

An autumnal spin on summer's basil and pine nut rendition, this pesto is delicious paired with grilled meats and is also an equally wonderful substitute for marinara sauce on a pizza topped with wild mushrooms and cubes of butternut squash or pie pumpkin.

½ c. chopped pecans, toasted
½ c. fresh flat-leaf parsley, packed
¼ c. fresh sage leaves, packed
¼ c. grated Parmesan cheese
¼ c. extra-virgin olive oil
1 t. lemon juice
1 clove garlic, chopped
¼ t. salt

Combine all ingredients in a food processor; process until ingredients are finely chopped. Makes ¾ cup.

Roast Pork with
Sage & Pecan Pesto

Sweet Potato Galette

Layers of nutmeg-spiced sweet potatoes make the ultimate fall comfort food.

**2 lbs. sweet potatoes, peeled and sliced into
⅛-inch thick rounds**
¼ c. butter, melted and divided
2 T. all-purpose flour
1 t. salt
½ t. pepper
¼ t. nutmeg

Combine sweet potatoes and 2 tablespoons butter in a large bowl, tossing to coat. Combine flour and next 3 ingredients; sprinkle over potatoes and toss to coat.

Place remaining 2 tablespoons butter in a 10" cast-iron skillet or other large ovenproof skillet. In the skillet, arrange sweet potatoes in a single layer, in slightly overlapping circles. Top with remaining sweet potatoes.

Cut a circle of nonstick aluminum foil; place over potatoes. Place a 9" cast-iron skillet on top of foil to weight the galette. Cook over medium heat for 5 minutes; don't remove cover. Transfer weighted skillet to oven; bake at 375 degrees for 10 minutes. Remove top skillet and foil; and bake 15 more minutes, or until potatoes are tender. Loosen edges with a spatula and invert onto a serving plate. Serves 6.

Green Beans Almondine

The fresh flavor of green beans really shines in this dish and the light sauce is more of a dressing.

2 T. butter
3 lbs. green beans, trimmed
3 c. chicken broth
½ t. pepper
2 T. cornstarch
¼ c. water
2 T. lemon juice
¼ c. slivered almonds, toasted

Melt butter in a large skillet over medium-high heat. Add beans and sauté 5 minutes. Add broth and pepper; bring to a boil. Reduce heat, cover and simmer 15 minutes. Dissolve cornstarch in water; add to skillet. Bring to a boil; cook one minute, stirring constantly. Stir in lemon juice. Sprinkle with almonds. Serves 12.

Ginger Streusel-Topped Cheesecake

This easy dressed-up cheesecake is topped with big chunks of crunchy gingersnap streusel. Scoop it warm from the oven into dessert bowls.

1 c. gingersnaps, coarsely crushed
½ c. butter, softened
½ c. sugar
½ c. all-purpose flour
Optional: 1 T. crystallized ginger, finely chopped
30-oz. frozen New York-style cheesecake

Combine first 5 ingredients, mixing well with a spoon. Sprinkle streusel over top of frozen cheesecake. Bake at 425 degrees for 16 to 19 minutes, or until streusel is golden. Scoop warm cheesecake into serving bowls. Serves 8.

Ginger Streusel-Topped Cheesecake

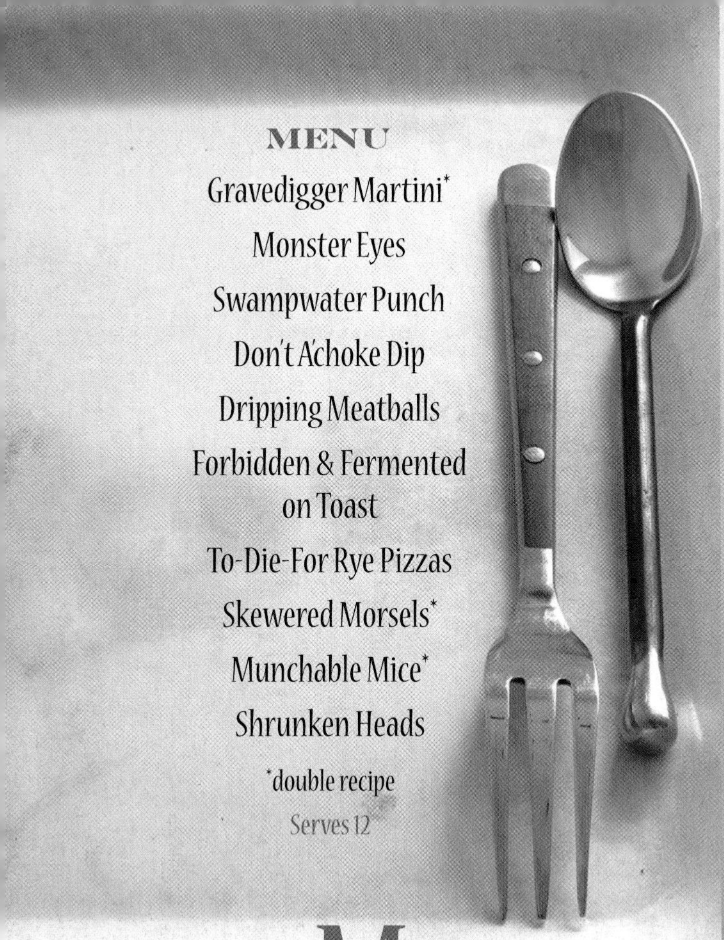

MENU

Gravedigger Martini*

Monster Eyes

Swampwater Punch

Don't A'choke Dip

Dripping Meatballs

Forbidden & Fermented
on Toast

To-Die-For Rye Pizzas

Skewered Morsels*

Munchable Mice*

Shrunken Heads

*double recipe

Serves 12

Masquerade Party

WHO SAYS HALLOWEEN IS CHILD'S PLAY? This gathering was created with adults in mind. Pass out decorated eye masks at the door and let the fun begin. Serve delicious nibbles masquerading as something more sinister. Ask guests to write one unknown fact about themselves on an adhesive nametag worn throughout the party, then let them try to figure out who's who.

[*Masquerading as a normal person day after day is exhausting.*]
—ANONYMOUS

Pour chocolate coating into a saucer. Dip the rims of 4 to 6 chilled martini glasses in coating; chill until set. In a pitcher, combine liqueur or milk, half-and-half and vodka, if using; set aside. Working in batches, fill a martini shaker with ice cubes, add liqueur mixture and shake. Strain into prepared glasses. Garnish as desired. Serves 4 to 6.

Monster Eyes

Beware...these silly sausage balls stare back!

3 c. biscuit baking mix
1 lb. ground mild or hot pork sausage
3½ c. shredded extra-sharp Cheddar
  cheese
54 small green olives with pimentos

Combine baking mix, sausage and cheese in a large bowl. Stir with a wooden spoon until blended.

Shape sausage mixture into one-inch balls and place on lightly greased baking sheets. Press one olive deeply into each ball. Reroll using the palms of your hands if you need to reshape. Bake at 400 degrees for 22 minutes, or until lightly golden. Makes about 4 ½ dozen.

TIP

Freeze Monster Eyes in an airtight container up to one month. To reheat, place frozen balls on ungreased baking sheets and bake at 350 degrees for 10 minutes, or until heated through.

Gravedigger
Martini

Gravedigger Martini

Deep, dark chocolate presented in a muddy martini. Mmmmm...cheers!

¾ c. hard-shell chocolate ice cream coating
1 c. chocolate liqueur or chocolate milk
¾ c. half-and-half
Optional: ¼ c. vodka
2 c. ice cubes
Garnishes: whipped cream, chocolate shavings

Monster Eyes

Don't A'choke Dip

Swampwater Punch

This green punch is replete with slimy swamp delicacies. Ewww!

**12-oz. can frozen orange juice concentrate,
    partially thawed**
1 qt. white grape juice
1 ½ c. water
5 drops green food coloring
2-ltr. bottle lemon-lime soda
Garnish: gummy worms or gummy frogs

Combine juices, water and food coloring in a large pitcher; chill. Arrange gummy worms or frogs in the bottom of a 5-cup ring mold. Fill mold with water; freeze until solid, 8 hours to overnight. At serving time, turn out ice ring and place in a punch bowl. Pour chilled juice mixture into punch bowl; slowly pour in soda. Serve immediately. Serves 15 to 20.

Don't A'choke Dip

Try this dip with veggies, toasted bread or pita chips… whatever the dipper, it's sure to disappear in a flash.

2 c. grated Parmesan cheese
2 c. shredded mozzarella cheese
1 c. mayonnaise
2 cloves garlic, minced
**16-oz. can artichokes, drained and finely
    chopped**
¼ c. green onions, chopped
assorted crackers

Combine all ingredients except onions and crackers in an 8"x8" baking pan; mix thoroughly and bake at 375 degrees for 45 minutes. Sprinkle with green onions; serve with crackers. Makes 7 cups.

Forbidden &
Fermented on Toast

Forbidden & Fermented on Toast

A buttery mixture of brown sugar and chopped walnuts tops sweet apple slices and savory cheese for an elegant appetizer with broad appeal. We used a combination of Granny Smith and Braeburn apples, but use your favorite. Fresh pears are a good option, too.

1 baguette, cut into ¼-inch-thick slices
½ c. brown sugar, packed
½ c. chopped walnuts
¼ c. butter, melted
13.2-oz. pkg. Brie cheese, thinly sliced
3 Granny Smith apples or Braeburn apples,
   cored and sliced

Arrange bread slices on an ungreased baking sheet; bake at 350 degrees until lightly toasted. Set aside.

Mix together sugar, walnuts and butter. Top each slice of bread with a cheese slice, an apple slice and one teaspoon brown sugar mixture. Bake at 350 degrees for 3 to 5 minutes, or until cheese melts. Makes about 2½ dozen.

Dripping Meatballs

For a party, keep these unusual meatballs warm in a slow cooker turned to the lowest setting.

1 lb. ground beef
1 c. herb-flavored dry bread crumbs
1 c. whole-berry cranberry sauce, divided
1 egg, beaten
1 ½ t. salt
½ t. pepper
1 t. dried basil
½ t. dried thyme
2 T. oil
1 c. beef broth
½ c. orange juice
1 T. all-purpose flour

Combine ground beef, bread crumbs, ½ cup cranberry sauce, egg and seasonings. Mix well; shape into one-inch balls. Cook in hot oil until browned, about 10 minutes; drain. Combine broth and remaining cranberry sauce in a saucepan; heat until gently boiling. Stir together juice and flour in a bowl until smooth; add to mixture in saucepan, stirring until thickened. Reduce heat; add meat-balls and simmer 15 to 20 minutes. Makes about 3 dozen.

To-Die-For Rye Pizzas

1 lb. ground pork sausage
1 lb. ground beef
16-oz. pkg. pasteurized process cheese spread,
   cubed
1 T. catsup
1 t. Worcestershire sauce
1 to 2 loaves sliced party rye

Brown sausage and beef in a large skillet over medium-high heat; drain. Add cheese and stir over low heat until melted. Add catsup and Worcester-shire sauce. Spoon meat mixture onto rye slices by tablespoonfuls; arrange on a lightly greased baking sheet. Bake at 350 degrees for 10 to 12 minutes, or until cheese bubbles and bread is crisp. Serves 12 to 15.

Skewered Morsels

These kabobs are a heartier offering of finger food fare. Definitely double or triple the recipe to suit your guest list.

¼ c. soy sauce
3 T. brown sugar, packed
3 T. white vinegar
½ t. garlic powder
½ t. seasoned salt
½ t. garlic-pepper seasoning
½ c. lemon-lime soda
2 lbs. beef sirloin steak, cut into 1 ½-inch cubes
2 green peppers, diced
2 yellow peppers, diced
8-ozs. pkg. mushrooms, stems removed
1 pt. cherry tomatoes

Combine soy sauce, brown sugar, vinegar, garlic powder, seasoned salt, garlic-pepper seasoning and soda in a medium bowl; mix well and set aside. Arrange steak in a large plastic zipping bag. Reserve ½ cup soy sauce mixture for basting; pour remaining in bag and seal. Refrigerate 8 hours or overnight.

Thread steak, peppers, mushrooms and tomatoes alternately onto skewers. Lightly grease cold grill rack. Grill kabobs over high heat (400 to 500 degrees) for 10 minutes, or to desired doneness. Baste frequently with reserved marinade during the last 5 minutes of cooking. Serves 6 to 8.

Munchable Mice

Munchable Mice

No haunted house would be complete without scurrying mice. We've caught a few to serve to our guests!

6-oz. pkg. semi-sweet chocolate chips
2 t. shortening
24 maraschino cherries with stems, well drained
24 milk chocolate drops
48 almond slices
Garnish: white and red gel icing

Melt chocolate chips and shortening in a double boiler over low heat; stir until smooth. To make each mouse, hold a cherry by the stem and dip into melted chocolate mixture. Set on wax paper; press a chocolate drop onto opposite side of cherry from stem. For ears, insert 2 almond slices between cherry and chocolate drop. If desired, pipe 2 white icing dots with red icing centers for eyes. Cover; keep refrigerated. Makes 2 dozen.

Shrunken Heads

These little fellows add the right touch of whimsy to your Halloween décor. Don't eat…unless you really want to!

8 small Granny Smith apples, peeled
1 c. lemon juice
1 T. salt
red licorice, cut into short lengths

Core apples and carve facial features.

Combine lemon juice and salt. Add apples; toss to coat. Let stand one minute. Drain; let stand at room temperature one week. Add licorice for hair. Makes 8.

Tuck a few "surprise" elements into your table arrangement and porch decor. Rubber mice, plastic spiders, and these shrunken heads add wicked whimsy to door pockets, pumpkin displays and centerpieces.

Shrunken Heads

entertaining outdoors

IF YOU INVITE THEM, THEY WILL COME

Don't limit the guest list due to the size of your table. You can get away with improvising outdoors. Two sawhorses topped with an old door can be disguised in an instant and accommodate the masses. Plus when the part is over the sawhorses can be collapsed and put away along with the door, so storing a big table isn't necessary.

PLAY DRESS UP

Think beyond Halloween costumes and give some thought to gussying up your tables too. Layer outdoor fabrics, traditional linens, oilcloth or disposable paper or plastic table toppers. Just make sure to weigh them down should a blustery October wind kick up. Tie mini pumpkins to the corners of the tablecloth as whimsical tablecloth hold-downs. Weight napkins and plates too. Polished stones are another natural find that work great.

LET IT GLOW, LET IT GLOW, LET IT GLOW

Even on a night that's frightful, candlelight can set a festive mood. On breezy evenings, cover candles with glass hurricanes or set them in jam jars to protect flickering flames. Battery powered votives provide worry-free illumination and last hours. Place them inside paper bag luminaries for an ethereal glow (see page 177).

PROVIDE COMFORT

Be prepared for whatever Mother Nature throws your way. Having a tent or outdoor umbrellas at the ready is a worthwhile luxury should rain or intense sunshine appear. A blowing fan keeps mosquitoes at bay and provides relief from the heat of Indian summer. Be sure to have sunscreen and bug spray available to those who need it. If it is cool, a heat source is a wonderful addition that adds ambience too. A chiminea, firepit, bonfire or outdoor fireplace are perfect for gathering around, but a portable kerosene heater works too.

ASK FOR A TREAT

Don't get tricked into thinking you can do it all yourself. Ask for help. Make a to-do list of all that needs to be done and then share the tasks with a friend or two. Set up several hours before the party begins. Don't forget a trashcan with extra bags, a lighter for candles, wipes for messes, and hand sanitizer. Butcher paper on kid-size tables along with buckets of crayons will keep them occupied and serve as a tablecloth that is easily tossed after the fun.

MENU

Spiced Lemonade

Cranberry Waldorf
Salad

Country-Style 3-Bean
Salad

Pulled Pork Barbecue
Sandwiches

Loaded Potato Packets*

Oozing Cherry Pies

Pumpkin Lattes*

*double recipe
Serves 8 to 10

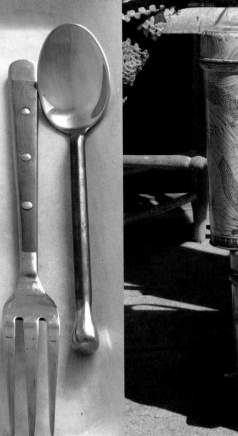

Pumpkin Patch Picnic

GATHER OUTDOORS to select the pick of the patch, then spend time together playing games, carving and decorating pumpkins and enjoying a country-size spread of delicious homemade offerings.

[*Give me a field where the* **unmow'd** *grass grows . . .*
—WALT WHITMAN]

Cranberry Waldorf
Salad

Spiced Lemonade

½ c. lemon juice
½ c. brown sugar, packed
½ t. vanilla extract
¼ t. cinnamon
⅛ t. nutmeg
⅛ t. ground cloves
⅛ t. allspice
10 c. warm water

Add all ingredients to a pitcher with a lid; shake
well. Set aside to cool to room temperature. Pour
through a coffee filter into another pitcher; discard
solids. Serve warm or cold. Serves 8 to 10.

Cranberry Waldorf Salad

*A traditional recipe with the added tartness of dried
cranberries...try it with almonds, too!*

2 c. Granny Smith apples, chopped
2 c. Red Delicious apples, chopped
juice of 3 lemons
½ c. celery, chopped
½ c. chopped walnuts
1 c. sweetened dried cranberries
½ c. grapes, halved
2 c. whipped cream
½ c. mayonnaise
¼ t. nutmeg

Combine apples, lemon juice, celery, walnuts,
cranberries and grapes in a large serving bowl; set
aside. Combine whipped cream and mayonnaise in
a medium bowl; mix well. Toss with apple mixture.
Sprinkle with nutmeg; chill before serving. Serves 8.

Country-Style 3-Bean Salad

This easy make-ahead recipe is a must-have for any large gathering.

14 ½-oz. can green beans, drained
14 ½-oz. can yellow wax beans, drained
15 ½-oz. can kidney beans, drained and rinsed
1 red onion, thinly sliced
¾ c. sugar
⅔ c. vinegar
⅓ c. oil
1 t. salt
¼ t. pepper
¼ t. dried oregano

Toss beans and onion together in a large bowl; set aside. Combine remaining ingredients in a small saucepan over medium heat. Cook and stir until sugar dissolves; pour over bean mixture. Cover and chill overnight. Serves 10 to 12.

Several weeks before your pumpkin patch is ready to harvest, choose a pumpkin that's deep orange in color. Don't pick the pumpkin…it has to continue to grow in the patch. Simply wipe it clean with a mild bleach and water solution and use a craft knife to write a greeting on the shell… the letters should only be carved about ⅛-inch deep. Now wipe the pumpkin clean again, and as the pumpkin grows, so will your message.

Pulled Pork Barbecue Sandwiches

Keep some of the Dry Rub Mix on hand for roasted or grilled dishes…it adds plenty of flavor to any recipe.

3- to 5-lb. boneless pork roast
Dry Rub Mix
1 to 2 T. olive oil
barbecue sauce to taste
8 to 12 sandwich buns

Rub surface of pork with Dry Rub Mix to taste, reserving the rest for another use. Heat oil over medium heat in a large skillet; brown pork on all sides.

Place the pork in a lightly greased roasting pan. Bake at 325 degrees for 3 to 3 ½ hours, or until very tender. When done, use 2 forks to shred meat. Add barbecue sauce to taste and serve on buns. Serves 8 to 12.

Dry Rub Mix:

½ c. paprika
¼ c. salt
¼ c. pepper
¼ c. brown sugar, packed
¼ c. chili powder
¼ c. ground cumin
1 T. cayenne pepper
1 t. onion powder
1 t. garlic powder

Combine all ingredients in a mixing bowl; blend well. Store in an airtight container. Makes 1¾ cups.

Set up a spot for kiddie tractor pulls around the pumpkin patch or yard. Hay bales serve as soft benches and add to the hayride feel.

Pulled Pork Barbecue Sandwiches

Loaded Potato Packets

Top servings with sour cream and sliced green onions...
oh-so good! These foil packs are great for baking ahead
and keeping warm en route to a picnic. You'll need
to double the recipe for this menu; make two packets
rather than one large one.

3 baking potatoes, peeled and thinly sliced
½ onion, thinly sliced
1 T. garlic, minced
½ t. dried parsley
salt and pepper to taste
4 slices bacon, crisply cooked, crumbled
   and 1 T. drippings reserved
2 T. butter, sliced
1 c. shredded Cheddar cheese

Arrange potatoes on half of a lightly greased 30-inch length of heavy-duty aluminum foil. Top with onion; sprinkle with garlic, parsley, salt and pepper. Drizzle with reserved drippings; add butter, crumbled bacon and cheese. Fold aluminum foil loosely over potatoes; seal edges of packet tightly. Place on a baking sheet; bake at 350 degrees for 30 to 35 minutes. Open carefully and check for doneness; return to oven for a few minutes longer, if necessary. Serves 4.

Oozing Cherry Pies

Oozing Cherry Pies

With a pie iron, you can make a truly scrumptious dessert over the campfire.

21-oz. can cherry pie filling
1 t. almond extract
1 pound cake or angel food cake, sliced ½-inch
  thick
softened butter
Garnish: powdered sugar

Combine pie filling and extract in a small bowl; set aside. Spread cake slices lightly on one side with butter. Place one cake slice buttered-side down in a cast-iron pie iron; top with one to 2 tablespoons pie filling mixture and a second cake slice, buttered-side up. Close pie iron; cook over a grill or campfire for 4 to 6 minutes, or until toasted and heated through. Sprinkle pie with powdered sugar; repeat with remaining cake slices and pie filling mixture. Serves 10 to 12.

Pumpkin Lattes

This creamy concoction is a delicious way to warm up on a brisk autumn day.

4 c. milk
¼ c. canned pumpkin
3 T. vanilla extract
1 t. cinnamon
2 c. hot, strong brewed coffee
Garnishes: whipped cream, pumpkin pie spice,
  cinnamon sticks
Chocolate-Dipped Spoons (see page 147)

Stir together milk and pumpkin in a saucepan; cook over low heat until steaming. Stir in vanilla and cinnamon. With a handheld blender or electric mixer, blend for 15 to 20 seconds, or until thick and foamy. Pour into 4 to 6 mugs or tall glasses; pour in hot coffee. If desired, top with whipped cream, sprinkle with spice and add cinnamon stick stirrers. Serve immediately. Serves 4 to 6.

Ooey, Gooey
S'mores

Tips for Making Ooey, Gooey S'mores

A wooden tool caddy lined with parchment paper makes a whimsical s'mores carrier...just fill with marshmallows, chocolate bars, graham crackers and assorted cookies. See page 136 for our homemade marshmallow recipe.

For fun, try a fresh twist on this campfire classic...

• Use chocolate or cinnamon-flavored graham crackers.

• Top graham crackers with peanut butter and jam before adding toasted marshmallows.

• Enjoy any of your favorite candy bars...a peanut butter cup or peppermint patty...heavenly!

• Layer with thinly sliced bananas or apples...so yummy with melted chocolate.

Fright Night Film Festival

HOST A HALLOWEEN FILM FESTIVAL every weekend in October. Check out the library or video store for old classics like *Frankenstein, The Mummy, Dracula* and *The Invisible Man.* Project the movies onto an outdoor wall or bed sheet. Stoke a grill or bonfire outdoors and serve inspired renditions of classic movie theater snacks.

[*Those who are easily shocked should be shocked more often.*
—MAE WEST]

Spiced Pear Cider

Triple this recipe for a crowd. If warm weather is predicted, prepare it a day in advance and chill. Serve it over crushed ice.

16 whole allspice berries
8 whole cloves
4 (3-inch) cinnamon sticks
6 c. unsweetened pear juice
2 c. pear nectar

Place allspice, cloves and cinnamon sticks in the center of a coffee filter or an 8-inch square of cheesecloth. Gather edges and tie with a small piece of kitchen string. Combine spice bag, pear juice and pear nectar in a 3-quart slow cooker. Cover and cook on low setting 3 hours. Remove and discard spice bag. Serve hot. Makes 8 cups.

ADMITS A CROWD

Four Weekends of Popcorn:

Harvest Moon Caramel Corn

Candy Corn Popcorn Balls

Red Cinnamon Popcorn

Nutty Popcorn Snack Mix

Spiced Pear Cider

Harvest Moon Caramel Corn

Turn ordinary microwave popcorn into an extraordinary caramel snack. Not only is it good for movie night, but it's also a good treat for giving...especially since it makes an abundant amount!

10½-oz. box microwave popcorn, popped
1 c. butter
2 c. brown sugar, packed
½ c. corn syrup
½ t. salt
1 t. vanilla extract
½ t. baking soda

Place popcorn in a lightly greased large roasting pan; set aside. Combine butter, brown sugar, corn syrup and salt in a heavy saucepan. Bring to a boil over medium heat; cook 5 minutes. Remove from heat. Add vanilla and baking soda; stir well and pour over popcorn. Mix well.

Bake at 250 degrees for one hour, stirring occasionally; let cool. Break into pieces and store in an airtight container. Makes 27 cups.

Candy Corn Popcorn Balls

50 large marshmallows
⅓ c. butter or margarine
20 c. freshly popped popcorn
2 c. teddy bear-shaped chocolate graham
    cracker cookies
2 ½ c. candy corn

Combine marshmallows and butter in a Dutch oven. Cook over medium-low heat until melted and smooth, stirring occasionally. Remove from heat.

Combine popcorn and cookies in a large bowl. Pour marshmallow mixture over popcorn mixture, tossing to coat. Stir in candy corn. Spray hands with vegetable spray and shape popcorn mixture into 3-inch balls, pressing together firmly. Cool on wax paper. Wrap balls in plastic wrap. Store in an airtight container up to 3 days. Makes 20.

Candy Corn
Popcorn Balls

Red Cinnamon Popcorn

6 qts. popped popcorn
12-oz. pkg. red cinnamon candies
sugar
1 c. butter
½ c. corn syrup
1 t. salt
½ t. baking soda

Spread popcorn in a lightly buttered roasting pan; bake at 250 degrees while preparing syrup, about 10 minutes. Pour cinnamon candies into a 2-cup measuring cup; fill remaining space to the top with sugar. Place in a heavy saucepan; add butter, corn syrup and salt. Bring to a boil; boil 5 minutes. Remove from heat; carefully stir in baking soda. Pour over warmed popcorn, stirring to coat. Bake at 250 degrees for one hour, stirring every 15 minutes. Remove from oven; let cool. Break into pieces; store in an airtight container. Makes 6 quarts.

Nutty Popcorn Snack Mix

16 c. popped popcorn
5 c. mini pretzel twists
2 c. brown sugar, packed
1 c. butter
½ c. dark corn syrup
½ t. salt
½ t. baking soda
1 t. vanilla extract
1 c. dry-roasted peanuts
2 c. candy corn or candy-coated chocolates

Combine popcorn and pretzels in a large roasting pan; set aside. Combine brown sugar, butter, corn syrup and salt in a heavy medium saucepan. Cook over medium heat 12 to 14 minutes, stirring occasionally, until mixture comes to a full boil. Continue cooking and stirring 4 to 6 minutes, until mixture reaches the soft-ball stage, or 234 to 243 degrees on a candy thermometer. Remove from heat; stir in baking soda and vanilla.

Pour over popcorn and pretzels in pan; add peanuts. Stir until mixture is coated well. Bake at 200 degrees for 20 minutes; stir. Bake for an additional 25 minutes. Immediately spoon onto wax paper; let cool completely. Break into pieces; store in an airtight container. Makes about 24 cups.

Roasted Corn with Rosemary Butter

Nothing tastes better than last-of-the-season sweet corn roasted in the husk. Hot buttered corn is street food in many places and is a perfectly portable and fresh alternative to popped corn.

12 ears yellow or white sweet corn, in husks
½ c. butter, softened
2 t. fresh rosemary, chopped

Pull back corn husks, leaving them attached. Remove and discard silks. Combine butter and rosemary in a small bowl; brush over corn. Pull husks over corn and grill over medium-high heat (350 to 400 degrees) for about 15 minutes, turning occasionally. Pull back husks and enjoy. Serves 12.

TIP
Insert corn holders, a skewer or even a sharpened stick into one end of the cob for ease of eating out of hand.

Best-Ever Soft Pretzels

Best-Ever Soft Pretzels

Enjoy these warm from the oven...there's nothing like them!

1 env. active dry yeast
1 ½ c. very warm water
1 T. sugar
2 t. salt
4 c. all-purpose flour
1 egg yolk
1 T. water
¼ c. coarse salt

In a large bowl, dissolve yeast in warm (110 degrees) water in a large bowl. Stir in sugar and salt until dissolved. Add flour; mix well. Turn onto a floured surface; knead 5 minutes. Divide dough into 16 equal pieces. Roll into thin strips; shape into pretzels. Place on a well-greased baking sheet. Beat egg yolk with water; brush on pretzels. Sprinkle with salt; bake at 425 degrees for 15 to 20 minutes, or until golden. Makes 16 pretzels.

Light the way with a path of glowing pumpkins. Use cookie or aspic cutters to punch patterns in the pumpkins' skin, then tuck strands of battery-powered lights inside each. Hide cords with pine needles or mulch.

Campfire Corn Dogs

An all-time favorite...corn dogs come out golden and delicious when prepared in a pie iron. It's always nice to have something hot for guests. These can be made three at a time, but they also hold well when kept warm.

8½-oz. pkg. corn muffin mix
8 to 10 hot dogs

Prepare corn muffin mix according to package directions; set aside. Place 3 hot dogs inside a well-greased cast-iron hot dog cooker or square pie iron. Pour in enough batter to fill the bottom of the cooker. Close cooker; turn over and cook over a grill or campfire 3 minutes. Turn over; cook an additional 3 minutes or until cornbread is set. Repeat with remaining batter and hot dogs. Slice between hot dogs to serve. Serves 8 to 10.

A photo booth is a fun addition and can be made from a refrigerator box. Decorate it with a Halloween theme. Cut out a window and let kids climb inside and make silly faces while you take their photo with a Polaroid camera for instant gratification and a souvenir of a fun time.

Film festival @ Vickie's

Shiny Red Candy Apples

As enticing as the shiny apple the witch offered Snow White...beware!

4 c. sugar
1 c. butter
¼ c. white vinegar
¼ c. boiling water
½ t. red food coloring
¼ c. red cinnamon candies
10 popsicle sticks
10 Granny Smith apples
ice water

Combine sugar, butter, vinegar, boiling water and food coloring in a large heavy metal saucepan. Cook over low heat until sugar dissolves. Increase heat to medium-high; boil without stirring about 10 minutes, until mixture reaches the hard-crack stage, or 290 to 310 degrees on a candy thermometer. Remove from heat; stir in cinnamon candies and let stand until bubbles subside.

Insert sticks into apples. Dip apples into mixture; swirl to coat and dip into ice water to harden candy coating. Place on a lightly buttered baking pan until set. Store in a cool, dry place. Serves 10.

Shiny Red
Candy Apples

MENU

Frothy Orange Punch

Chocolatey Pumpkin Cookies

Black Cat Cut-Out Cookies

Melted Witches

Poisoned Pecan Squares

Green Gobblin' Cookies

Crescent Moons

Ghosts in the Mud

Serves 6 to 8

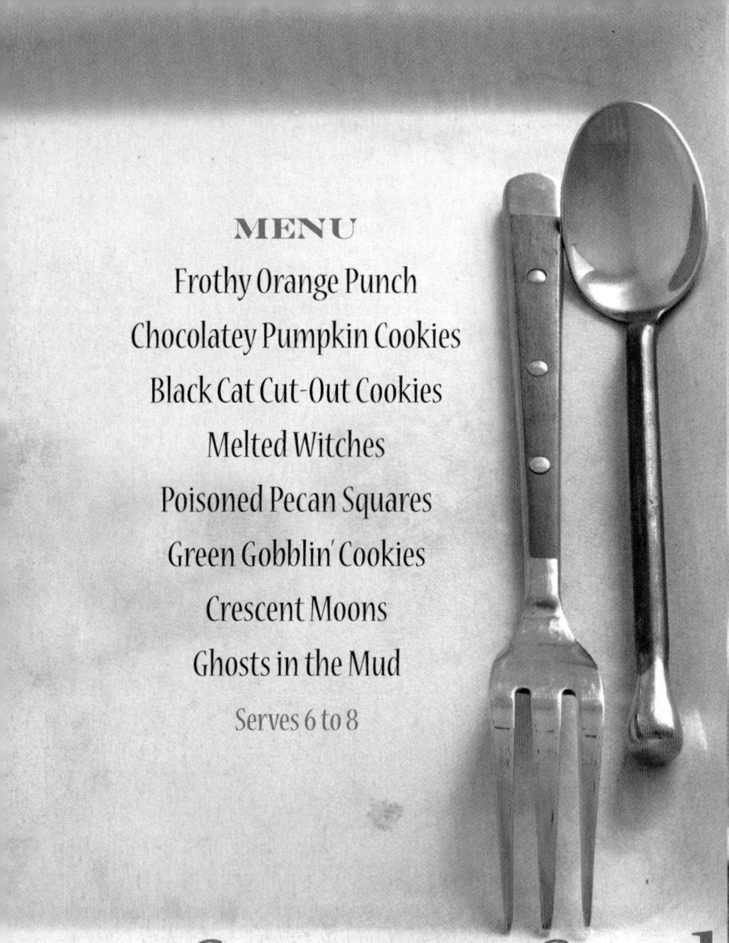

Creepy Cookie Swap

HOST A CREEPY-THEMED COOKIE SWAP to boost anticipation of Halloween. Send out invitations on different recipe cards printed from the assortment on the following pages…or tell guests to bring their own haunting home-made sweet. Showcase all the cookies on the table and after mingling and enjoying refreshments, start the swap. Move around the table in a clockwise direction, filling treat bins with a sampling of each frightfully delicious delight.

All seasons are sweet, but autumn is best of all.
—ELINOR WYLIE

Chocolatey Pumpkin Cookies

With their pumpkin flavor and hint of cinnamon, these cookies are the ideal October treat.

1 c. sugar
1 c. shortening
1 c. canned pumpkin
1 egg
1 t. vanilla extract
2 c. all-purpose flour
1 t. baking soda
½ t. salt
1 t. cinnamon
1 c. semi-sweet chocolate chips

Beat sugar and shortening at medium speed with an electric mixer until creamy. Add pumpkin, egg and vanilla, beating until blended; set aside.

Combine flour, baking soda, salt and cinnamon in a small bowl; gradually add to shortening mixture, beating well. Fold in chocolate chips.

Drop by tablespoonfuls onto ungreased baking sheets. Bake at 350 degrees for 15 to 20 minutes, or until bottoms are golden. Remove to wire racks to cool. Drizzle cookies with Brown Sugar Glaze. Makes 2 dozen.

Brown Sugar Glaze:

½ c. brown sugar, packed
3 T. butter
3 T. milk
1½ c. powdered sugar

Combine brown sugar, butter and milk in a small saucepan. Bring mixture to a boil over medium heat; boil 2 minutes. Remove from heat. Add powdered sugar. Beat at medium speed with an electric mixer until mixture is smooth.

Chocolatey Pumpkin Cookies

Frothy Orange Punch

The orange flavor is so refreshing...kids big & little will love this.

2 pts. vanilla ice cream, softened
2 pts. orange sherbet, softened
4 c. milk
2 c. orange soda, chilled

Scoop ice cream and sherbet into a punch bowl. Pour in milk and soda; stir gently. Serve immediately. Serves 15 to 20.

Black Cat
Cut-Out Cookies

Store-bought fortune cookies dipped in chocolate offer up warnings to guests. Print and insert funny "misfortunes" to amuse your guests.

You shouldn't have trusted the cook!

Eat, Drink and Be War

Black Cat Cut-Out Cookies

Fun for goblins of all ages to make!

1 c. butter, softened
⅔ c. sugar
1 egg
1 t. vanilla extract
2½ c. all-purpose flour
Garnishes: black sanding sugar, small candies

Blend together butter and sugar; stir in egg and vanilla. Add flour; mix until well blended. Shape into a ball; cover and chill 4 hours to overnight. Roll out dough ¼-inch thick on a lightly floured surface; cut out with cat-shaped cookie cutters.

Arrange cookies on lightly greased baking sheets; bake at 350 degrees for 8 to 10 minutes, or until golden. Frost cookies with Chocolate Frosting when cool; if desired, sprinkle with black sanding sugar and add candy "eyes." Makes about 2 dozen.

Chocolate Frosting:

2¼ c. powdered sugar
3 T. butter, melted
3 T. milk
1 T. vanilla extract
1½ t. lemon juice
2 to 3 T. baking cocoa

Combine all ingredients in a medium bowl. Beat with an electric mixer on low speed until smooth.

Melted Witches

½ c. sugar
½ c. brown sugar, packed
½ c. creamy peanut butter
¼ c. butter, softened
¼ c. shortening
1 egg
1¼ c. all-purpose flour
½ t. baking soda
½ t. baking powder
¼ t. salt
milk chocolate drops

In a large bowl, blend sugars, peanut butter, butter, shortening and egg. Stir in remaining ingredients. Cover and chill for 2 hours, or until firm. Form dough into one-inch balls; place 1½ inches apart on ungreased baking sheets. Make an indentation in each ball with your thumb. Bake at 375 degrees for 9 to 10 minutes, or until lightly golden. Remove the pan from the oven and press a chocolate drop into the center of each. Cool two minutes on baking sheets. Remove to wire rack to cool completely. Makes 2 ½ to 3 dozen.

Melted Witches

Make containers for your guests to take cookies home. Tall tumblers or small galvanized pails are the perfect shape for protecting cookies in transport. Decorate the outside with painted designs. Be sure to personalize with guests' names and tuck a "thank you" note inside.

Poisoned Pecan Squares

Poisoned Pecan Squares

...just kidding, my little pretty!

2 c. all-purpose flour
⅔ c. powdered sugar
1⅓ c. plus 1 T butter, divided
½ c. brown sugar, packed
½ c. honey
3 T. whipping cream
3 ½ c. pecans, coarsely chopped

Sift together flour and powdered sugar. Cut in ¾ cup softened butter using a pastry blender or fork just until mixture resembles coarse crumbs meal. Pat mixture on bottom and 1½ inches up sides of a lightly greased 13"x9" baking pan.

Bake at 350 degrees for 20 minutes, or until edges are lightly golden. Cool. In a saucepan over medium-high heat, bring brown sugar, honey, ⅔ cup butter, and whipping cream to a boil. Stir in pecans and pour into prepared crust.

Bake at 350 degrees for 25 to 30 minutes, or until golden and bubbly. Cool in pan on a wire rack. Cut into 2-inch squares. Makes about 28 squares.

Crescent Moons

Remember your littlest guests with a photo snapped on the scene. Frame with a mat decorated with Halloween stickers or découpage candy wrappers.

Green Gobblin' Cookies

With only a few ingredients, you can transform break-fast cereal into crunchy green cookies fit for a goblin... or just plain gobbling.

12-oz. pkg. white melting chocolate
green paste food coloring
2½ c. mini shredded whole-wheat cereal
  biscuits, coarsely crushed

Microwave chocolate in a microwave-safe bowl on medium for 3 minutes, stirring after every minute. Stir in desired amount of food coloring. Add cereal, stirring gently to coat. Drop cereal mixture by heaping tablespoonfuls onto wax paper. Let cookies stand about 30 minutes, or until firm. Makes about 1½ dozen.

Crescent Moons

1 c. butter, softened
2¾ c. powdered sugar, divided
2 t. vanilla extract
1 c. pecan halves, toasted and finely ground
2½ c. all-purpose flour
2 c. powdered sugar

Beat butter and ¾ cup powdered sugar at medium speed with an electric mixer until creamy. Stir in vanilla and pecans. Gradually add flour, beating until a soft dough forms. Cover and chill one hour.

Divide dough into 5 portions; divide each portion into 12 pieces. Roll dough pieces into 2-inch logs, curving ends to form crescents. Place on ungreased baking sheets.

Bake at 350 degrees for 10 to 12 minutes, or until lightly golden. Cool on baking sheets 5 minutes. Roll warm cookies in 2 cups powdered sugar. Cool completely on wire racks. Roll cookies in remaining powdered sugar. Makes about 5 dozen.

Ghosts in the Mud

These cookies are so ooey-gooey and chocolatey that a gang of ghosts couldn't resist and got stuck!

1 c. semisweet chocolate chips
½ c. butter, softened
1 c. sugar
2 eggs
1 t. vanilla extract
1½ c. all-purpose flour
1 t. baking powder
½ t. salt
1 c. chopped pecans
½ c. milk chocolate chips
1 c. plus 2 T. mini marshmallows

Microwave semisweet chocolate morsels in a microwave-safe bowl on high for one minute, or until smooth, stirring every 30 seconds.

Beat butter and sugar at medium speed with an electric mixer until creamy; add eggs, one at a time, beating well after each addition. Beat in vanilla and melted chocolate.

Combine flour, baking powder and salt; gradually add to chocolate mixture, beating until well blended. Stir in chopped pecans and milk chocolate chips. Drop dough by heaping tablespoonfuls onto parchment paper-lined baking sheets. Press 3 marshmallows into each cookie.

Bake at 350 degrees for 10 to 12 minutes, or until set. Remove to wire racks to cool completely. Makes about 3 dozen.

Send kids a lunchbox surprise. Slip cookies inside vellum envelopes and tie them closed with shoestring licorice!

Ghosts in the Mud

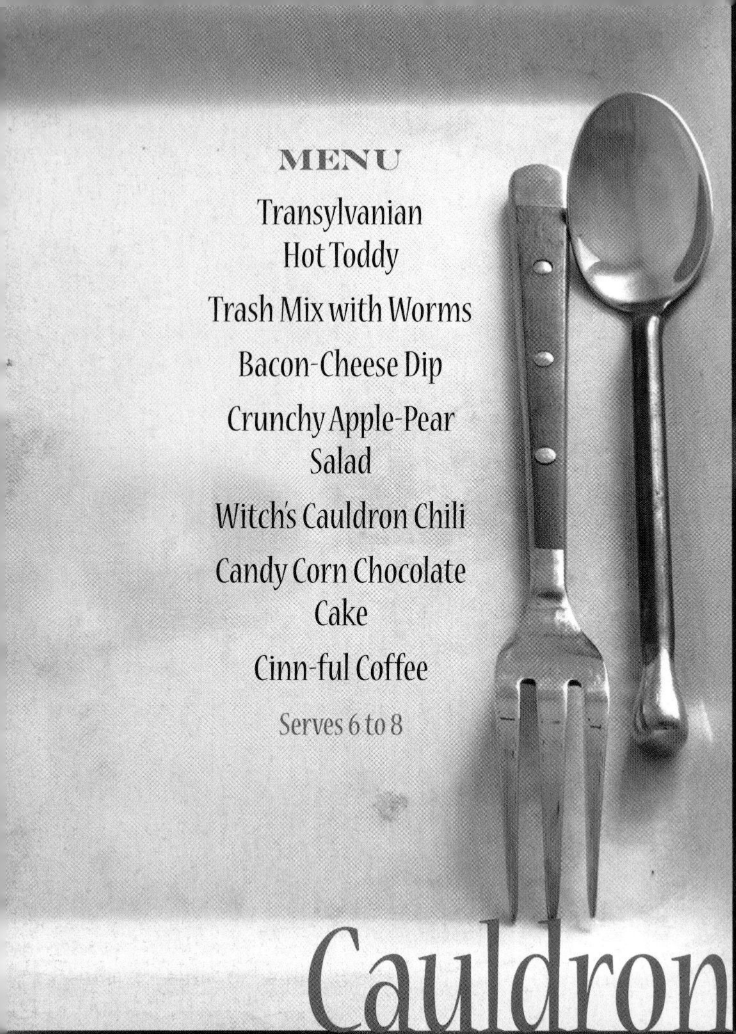

MENU

Transylvanian
Hot Toddy

Trash Mix with Worms

Bacon-Cheese Dip

Crunchy Apple-Pear
Salad

Witch's Cauldron Chili

Candy Corn Chocolate
Cake

Cinn-ful Coffee

Serves 6 to 8

Cauldronluck

POTLUCKS ARE ONE OF THE EASIEST ways to entertain. Everyone shares in the cooking and takes home their dish for clean-up. After a night of trick-or-treating folks can meet back at the house on the screened porch to sort candy, tell ghost stories and enjoy a bubbling hot meal certain to be the envy of witches everywhere.

The whole neighborhood abounds with *local tales,*
haunted spots and *twilight* superstitions.
—WASHINGTON IRVING

Transylvanian
Hot Toddy

Trash Mix with Worms

This is a fun mix to package in cellophane treat bags and give away on Halloween night. Change the fillings to suit your tastes…add more savory bits like cheese squares and cereal. Change the candy pieces to suit the season…red and green candy-coated chocolate pieces around the holidays and pastel-hued treats in spring.

16-oz. pkg. candy corn
15-oz. pkg. pretzel nuggets
12-oz. pkg. caramel popcorn and peanuts
15-oz. pkg. banana chips
15-oz. pkg. candy-coated chocolate pieces
15-oz. pkg. dried mango
15-oz. pkg. dried pineapple
10-oz. pkg. toffee pretzels
6-oz. pkg. sweetened dried cranberries
6-oz. pkg. gummy worms

Stir together all ingredients. Store in an airtight container. Makes 16 cups.

Trash Mix with
Worms

Transylvanian
Hot Toddy

This lemonade takes away the goose bumps and smoothes raised hairs.

4 c. water
3 c. fresh lemon juice (about 13 lemons)
1¾ to 2 c. sugar
¼ c. honey
Garnish: cinnamon sticks
Optional: dark rum

Combine first 4 ingredients in a 3- or 3 ½-quart slow cooker.

   Cover and cook on low setting 3 hours, or until thoroughly heated. Whisk well before serving. Serve warm with cinnamon sticks and a shot of dark rum, if desired. Makes 9 cups.

Cruncy Apple-Pear
Salad

Bacon-Cheese Dip

Beware...this dip is highly addictive!

1 lb. bacon, crisply cooked and crumbled
2 (8-oz.) pkgs. finely shredded Cheddar cheese
2 c. mayonnaise
1 c. chopped pecans
Optional: ½ c. onion, finely chopped
assorted crackers

Mix together all ingredients except crackers; chill.
Serve with crackers. Makes 6 to 7 cups.

Crunchy Apple-Pear Salad

2 apples, cored and diced
2 pears, cored and thinly sliced
1 T. lemon juice
2 heads butter lettuce, torn into bite-size pieces
½ c. crumbled Gorgonzola cheese
½ c. chopped walnuts, toasted

Toss apples and pears with lemon juice; drain.
Arrange lettuce on 6 salad plates; top with apples,
pears and Gorgonzola cheese. Drizzle salads with
Dressing; sprinkle with walnuts. Serve immediately. Serves 6.

Dressing:

1 c. oil
6 T. cider vinegar
½ c. sugar
1 t. celery seed
½ t. salt
¼ t. pepper

Combine all ingredients in a jar with a tightly fitting lid; cover. Shake well until dressing is blended
and sugar dissolves. Keep refrigerated.

Witch's Cauldron Chili

Prepare up to two days in advance and refrigerate. Reheat over low heat, stirring frequently. If it's too thick, stir in a little water.

1 T. butter or margarine
3 carrots, peeled and chopped
1 onion, chopped
1 t. garlic, minced
4-lb. deli roast chicken, skinned, boned and
   coarsely chopped
2 (14-oz.) cans chicken broth
4 ½-oz. can chopped green chiles
1 t. ground cumin
⅛ t. ground red pepper
3 (16-oz.) cans great Northern beans, rinsed
   and drained
½ c. whipping cream
Optional: ¼ c. fresh cilantro, chopped

Melt butter in a Dutch oven over low heat; add carrot, onion and garlic. Sauté until tender.

Stir in chicken, chicken broth, green chiles, cumin and red pepper; bring to a boil over medium-high heat. Reduce heat, cover, and simmer 20 minutes.

In a bowl, mash beans using a potato masher until about half the beans are still whole. Add beans and whipping cream to chicken mixture. Cook 10 minutes over medium heat, stirring frequently, until thickened and hot. Stir in cilantro, if desired. Serves 8.

Candy Corn Chocolate Cakes

2 c. sugar
2 c. all-purpose flour
1 c. baking cocoa
1 c. oil
1 t. salt
2 eggs
1 c. buttermilk
1 c. hot water
2 t. baking soda
2 t. vanilla extract

Beat first 6 ingredients in a large bowl at medium speed with an electric mixer until blended. Stir in buttermilk.

Stir together one cup hot water and baking soda; stir into batter. Stir in vanilla. Pour into 2 greased and floured 9" round cake pans.

Bake at 350 degrees for 30 to 40 minutes, or until a wooden pick inserted in center comes out

Witch's Cauldron Chili

Cinn-ful Coffee

A perfect warm ending to a meal and just what you need before stepping back out into the dark! Make a full pot of coffee then add the amounts listed below to each for the perfect, spiced cupful.

1 c. hot, strong brewed coffee
1 T. grated semi-sweet chocolate
Optional: 3 T. coffee liqueur
whipped cream
Garnish: cinnamon stick

Combine coffee, chocolate and liqueur, if using, in a large cup or mug; stir until chocolate melts. Dollop with whipped cream. Garnish with cinnamon stick, if desired. Makes about 1¼ cups.

Candy Corn Chocolate
Cakes

Cinn-ful Coffee

clean. Cool in pans on wire racks 10 minutes. Remove from pans and cool completely on wire racks.

Freeze layers 30 minutes. Cut each layer into 8 wedges. Pipe Buttercream Frosting on top and sides of cake wedges to resemble candy corn. Using a medium star tip, pipe white frosting on the small end of each cake, yellow frosting on center and orange on wide end. Serves 16.

Buttercream Frosting

1 c. butter or margarine, softened
2-lb. pkg. powdered sugar
⅓ c. milk
1 t. vanilla extract
orange paste food coloring
yellow paste food coloring

Beat butter at medium speed with an electric mixer until fluffy; gradually add powdered sugar, beating until light and fluffy. Add milk, beating until spreading consistency. Stir in vanilla.

Stir orange food coloring into 1½ cups frosting. Stir yellow food coloring into 1¼ cups frosting. Makes 3½ cups.

MENU

Crunchy Batwings

Fruit Swords with Ant Dip

Scary Sandwich Platter:

Black Cat Grilled Cheeses

Ham on Ghosts

Turkey Fingers

Spoiled Milk

Spooky Spiderweb Cupcakes

Serves 16 to 20

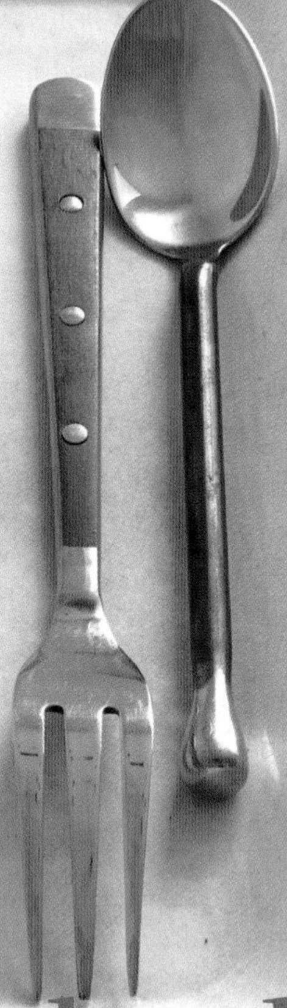

Scary School Party

GO WILD THIS HALLOWEEN and host the best party of the school year. Healthy foods go in disguise in this child-pleasing menu. Turn off the classroom lights and read an old ghost story or some Halloween history to keep them entertained… and eating.

A grandmother pretends she doesn't know
who you are on *Halloween.*
—ERMA BOMBECK

Crunchy Batwings

This is a fun substitute for the more expected potato chips. Once cool, store these in an airtight tin to keep them crisp.

2 c. bowtie pasta, uncooked
⅓ c. yellow cornmeal
3 T. Cajun seasoning
oil for deep frying

Cook pasta according to package directions; drain well and blot pasta dry with paper towels.

Combine cornmeal and Cajun seasoning in a large bowl. Toss pasta, a handful at a time, in cornmeal mixture to coat; shake off excess.

Pour oil to a depth of 2 inches in a Dutch oven; heat over medium-high heat to 375 degrees. Fry pasta, in batches, 3 to 4 minutes or until golden. Drain on paper towels. Store pasta snacks up to a week in an airtight container. Makes 6 cups.

Fruit Swords with
Ant Dip

Fruit Swords with
Ant Dip

*A few ants never hurt anything…especially when
you have a sword to protect you!*

2 c. pineapple, cubed
2 c. apple chunks, cubed
2 c. strawberries, halved
2 c. melon, cubed
2 c. vanilla yogurt
2 t. poppy seed

Thread fruit onto short plastic cocktail swords.
Combine yogurt and poppy seed and serve dip
alongside fruit. Serves 18 to 20.

When all else fails, think BLACK to set
the scene…black napkins, paper plates,
forks and spoons. Dark-purple drink mix
in clear plastic cups is an eerie sipper. Fill
cellophane goodie bags with black plastic
spider rings and tiny bottles of bubbles
disguised as something icky. Glue on copies of the "Embalming Fluid" label
(see page 189).

Ham on
Ghosts

Turkey
Fingers

Black Cat Grilled
Cheeses

Scary Sandwich Platter

Kids will get a kick out of these fun-shaped sandwiches! An assortment of fillings is sure to please even finicky feasters. Bread cutouts are great toasted and served as croutons for floating in soups or as surprising toppers for salads.

Black Cat Grilled Cheeses

24 slices pumpernickel bread
12 slices American cheese
butter

Cut cat shapes out of bread slices using a 3- to 4-inch cat-shaped cookie cutter. Cut the same shape from the cheese slices. Sandwich the cat-shaped cheese between two cat-shaped bread slices. Butter the outside of the sandwich and cook in a nonstick pan over medium-high heat for 2 minutes on each side, until toasted. Repeat using remaining bread and cheese. Makes 12 sandwiches.

Ham on Ghosts

24 slices white bread
12 slices deli ham
honey mustard

Cut ghost shapes out of bread slices using a 3- to 4-inch ghost-shaped cookie cutter. Cut the same shape from the cheese slices. Sandwich the ghost-shaped cheese between 2 cat-shaped bread slices that have been spread lightly with honey mustard. Repeat with remaining bread and ham. Makes 12 sandwiches.

Turkey Fingers

8 slices honey-wheat bread, crusts removed
20 thin slices deli turkey
ranch dressing

Cut bread slices into 4"x3" rectangles. Place several thin slices turkey on 4 rectangles of bread that have been spread lightly with ranch dressing. Spread a thin layer of ranch dressing on one side of each remaining rectangle of bread and top the sandwiches. Cut each sandwich in half. Makes 16 sandwiches.

Spoiled Milk

If you're using milk from the school cafeteria, be sure to bring clear plastic cups for this fun trick! This surprise must be made-to-order.

3 drops green food coloring
8 ounces milk
straws

Put 3 drops green food coloring in the bottom of a clear cup. Pour in milk and watch it "spoil"! Makes 1 serving.

Spoiled Milk

Fill miniature painted treat pails with an assortment of useful Halloween treats. Arrange them on the table to make an abundant and colorful centerpiece.

Spooky Spiderweb
Cupcakes

Spooky Spiderweb Cupcakes

*Don't worry about making the "webs" perfect...the more
imperfect, the spookier the effect.*

18¼-oz. pkg. chocolate or spice cake mix
½ c. semi-sweet chocolate chips
16-oz. container vanilla or orange frosting

Prepare cake mix according to package directions.
Bake in 18 to 24 paper-lined muffin cups. Cool and
set aside. Place chocolate chips in a small plastic
zipping bag; microwave on high 30 seconds to
one minute, or until melted. Snip off one corner of
bag to form a small hole; squeeze chocolate onto a
wax paper-lined baking sheet to form 3 concentric
circles. Immediately draw a toothpick through
circles to form spiderweb design. Repeat with
remaining chocolate; chill until set. Frost cupcakes;
press webs gently into frosting. Makes 18 to 24.

Embellish store-bought cupcakes
to save time too. Prepared frosting
makes it easy to create ghostly
mounds of goodness. Write "Boo"
on parchment paper using melted
chocolate then carefully remove
and use the letters to accent
your creations.

MENU

Dinner:

Candy Apple Punch

Fried Goo with
Dracula Dip

Sloppy Foes

Broccoli Parmesan

Halloween Sandwich
Cookies

Breakfast:

Hot Cocoa Supreme

Citrusy French Toast

Brown-Sugared Bacon

Cheesy Hashbrown Potatoes

Silly Yogurt Faces

Serves 6 to 8

Never-Slumber Party

Candy Apple Punch,
page 122

INVITE YOUR BEST PALS to a sleepless soiree with their teddy bears and pillows in tow. It will be a night of tall tales and fun… and lots of good food, too! After dinner, gather on the bed or around the fire and swap the scariest stories you know. When the sun comes up, a warm breakfast will chase away any lingering bad spirits.

So unfamiliar in the white moon-gleam, so old and ghostly like a house of dream . . .
—WILFRID WILSON GIBSON

Fried Goo With
Dracula Dip

Fried Goo With Dracula Dip

Just about everyone loves fried cheese sticks. Our version gets a punch of heat from cayenne pepper and cheese spiced with jalapeños. To tame the heat, use plain Monterey Jack (without the peppers), mozzarella or Swiss cheese and either leave out the cayenne pepper or use less of it.

2 (8-oz.) pkgs. Monterey Jack cheese with
   jalapeño peppers
1 c. all-purpose flour
1½ t. cayenne pepper
1 c. dry bread crumbs
1 t. dried parsley
4 eggs, beaten
oil for deep frying
Optional: marinara sauce

Cut cheese crosswise into ¾-inch slices. Lay slices flat and cut in half lengthwise.

Combine flour and cayenne pepper; stir well. Combine bread crumbs and parsley in another bowl; stir well. Dip cheese sticks in beaten eggs. Dredge in flour mixture. Dip coated cheese in egg again; dredge in bread crumb mixture, pressing firmly so that crumbs adhere. Place cheese sticks on a wax paper-lined baking sheet and freeze at least 30 minutes.

Heat 2 inches of oil in a Dutch oven to 375 degrees. Fry cheese sticks until golden. Drain on paper towels. Serve immediately with marinara sauce, if desired. Makes 28.

NOTE

Down to the wire? Prepare a store-bought package of frozen cheese sticks according to instructions and serve with warmed jarred marinara sauce.

GHOST STORIES should be age-appropriate for those gathered. Get good ideas from your local library or websites. See resources on page 201.

Candy Apple Punch

The sweet-and-sour potion will tattoo your tongue red.

6 c. cranberry-apple drink
3 c. water
15 hard cinnamon candies
6-oz. can limeade concentrate, thawed

Combine all ingredients in a large pitcher. Cover and chill 8 hours or until candies are dissolved. Pour mixture into a large Dutch oven and cook over medium heat until thoroughly heated. Serves 10.

Sloppy Foes

If you can't beat 'em, eat 'em. This sandwich is hardly your enemy. It might just become one of your favorite kid-pleasing meals.

1 lb. ground beef
1 onion, chopped
1 c. catsup
¼ c. water
2 T. Worcestershire sauce
¼ t. salt
1 t. pepper
6 to 8 sandwich buns

Brown ground beef and onion in a large skillet over medium-high heat, stirring until beef crumbles and is no longer pink; drain. Stir in catsup, water, Worcestershire sauce, salt and pepper; simmer 20 minutes, stirring frequently. Spoon onto buns. Serves 6 to 8.

Sloppy Foes

Broccoli Parmesan

This recipe calls for just broccoli flowerets, but don't discard the leaves and stalks. Instead, dice or shred them to use in salads and stir-fries.

8 c. broccoli flowerets
2 T. butter
3 T. onion, chopped
2 T. all-purpose flour
1 t. chicken bouillon granules
1¾ c. milk
½ c. grated Parmesan cheese
½ t. salt
½ t. pepper
½ t. dry mustard
¼ t. ground marjoram
Optional: additional Parmesan cheese

Steam broccoli, covered, in a steamer basket over boiling water 5 minutes or until crisp-tender. Keep warm.

Meanwhile, melt butter in a heavy saucepan; add onion and sauté until tender. Add flour and bouillon granules, stirring until blended. Cook, stirring constantly, one minute. Gradually add milk; cook over medium heat, stirring constantly, until thickened and bubbly. Stir in ½ cup cheese and next 4 ingredients; pour over broccoli. Sprinkle with additional cheese, if desired. Serves 6 to 8.

Halloween Sandwich Cookies

Use Halloween cookie cutters for fun shapes to sandwich the creamy filling of these delicious treats.

2 c. all-purpose flour
1 c. butter, softened
⅓ c. whipping cream
sugar to taste

Beat flour, butter and cream at medium speed with an electric mixer until combined; chill one hour.

Roll dough to ⅛- to ¼-inch thickness on a lightly floured surface. Cut with mini cookie cutters; place close together on ungreased baking sheets. Pierce each cookie several times with a fork; sprinkle lightly with sugar. Bake at 375 degrees for about 8 minutes, or until golden. Remove to wire racks to cool completely. Spread Creamy Filling between cookies, forming sandwiches. Makes about 4½ dozen.

Creamy Filling:

¼ c. butter, softened
¾ c. powdered sugar
1 t. vanilla extract

Beat butter at medium speed with an electric mixer until creamy; gradually add sugar, beating well. Stir in vanilla.

Hot Cocoa Supreme

Citrusy French Toast

To keep the cooked French toast slices warm while you're making more, place them on a baking sheet in a 300 degree oven. That way everyone can sit down and eat breakfast at the same time.

2 c. pancake mix
2 c. water
4 t. grated orange zest
4 T. powdered sugar
½ c. butter, divided
16 slices white sandwich bread
maple syrup

Whisk first 5 ingredients in a medium bowl until smooth.

Melt one tablespoon butter in a skillet over medium heat. Dip bread slices in the batter, coating well. Cook in batches 1 to 2 minutes on each side or until golden, turning with a spatula. Remove from pan; keep warm. Serve warm with maple syrup. Serves 8.

Brown-Sugared Bacon

This morning treat is the perfect mixture of salty and sweet.

½ c. brown sugar, packed
1 t. cinnamon
8 slices thick-sliced bacon, halved

Combine sugar and cinnamon in a small bowl. Dip each piece of bacon into mixture to coat. Twist each piece and arrange in an aluminum foil-lined broiler pan. Bake at 350 degrees for 15 to 20 minutes, or until bacon is crisp and sugar is bubbly. Place bacon on aluminum foil to cool. Makes 16 pieces.

Hot Cocoa Supreme

Topped with marshmallows and chocolate chips or even sprinkled with crushed mints, it's a terrific way to warm up.

¾ c. sugar
½ c. baking cocoa
¼ t. salt
5 c. water
2 c. milk
1 c. whipping cream
1 t. vanilla extract

Combine sugar, cocoa and salt in a saucepan; whisk in water. Bring to a boil over high heat, stirring until sugar is completely dissolved. Reduce heat to medium; add milk, cream and vanilla. Heat through without boiling; keep warm over low heat. Serves 6 to 8.

Citrusy French
Toast

Brown-Sugared
Bacon

Cheesy Hashbrown
Potatoes

Cheesy Hashbrown Potatoes

24-oz. pkg. frozen diced potatoes
2 c. shredded Colby cheese
¼ c. onion, minced
1 c. half-and-half or milk
½ c. beef broth
2 T. butter, melted
1 t. salt
¼ t. pepper
⅛ t. garlic powder
Garnish: crisply cooked and crumbled bacon

Combine frozen potatoes, cheese and onion in a large bowl; set aside. Mix remaining ingredients in a separate bowl; stir into potato mixture until well blended. Spoon into a greased 13"x9" baking pan. Bake, uncovered, at 425 degrees for 45 to 60 minutes. Garnish with bacon, if desired. Serves 8 to 10.

Silly Yogurt Faces

Look how easy it is to go from a plain yogurt to fancy faces! The sky's the limit when it comes to edible choices for funny facial features. Use those pictured or be creative and discover your own.

16-oz. container plain Greek yogurt
Decorations: cereal, grapes, blueberries, orange
   slices, strawberries, kiwi, gumdrops

Silly Yogurt Faces

tantalizing treats

GATHER TOGETHER TO MAKE YOUR OWN
Halloween delights…wrap up homemade
pops for trick-or-treaters or create a s'more
smorgasbord for a party host by filling a basket
with homemade marshmallows, graham
crackers and all the fixin's.

[*Danger and delight grow on one stalk.*
ENGLISH PROVERB]

Cake standing in for scoops of ice cream and lollipops made of cookie dough make these unexpected treats sure to elicit smiles!

Ice-Cream Cone Cakes

Ice-Cream Cone Cakes

Surprise your guests, kids in the classroom, or the birthday honoree with cake made in ice-cream cones. Everything is edible, and there are no forks & plates to clean up!

⅔ c. all-purpose flour
1 t. baking powder
⅛ t. salt
⅓ c. baking cocoa
2 T. butter, softened
½ c. sugar
⅔ c. buttermilk
½ t. vanilla extract
1 egg white
10 flat-bottomed ice-cream cones
Optional: colored sprinkles, 10 maraschino
  cherries with stems

Combine first 4 ingredients in a small bowl; set aside.

Beat butter and sugar in a large mixing bowl at medium speed with an electric mixer until creamy. Add flour mixture and buttermilk alternately to butter mixture, beginning and ending with flour mixture; beat at low speed after each addition just until blended. Stir in vanilla. Add egg white, mixing well.

Fill cones to within ½ inch of the top; carefully place on an ungreased baking sheet. Bake at 375 degrees for 35 minutes; cool completely on wire racks. Spread evenly with Frosting. Top with colored sprinkles and a cherry, if desired. Serves 10.

Frosting:

2 T. butter, softened
1½ c. powdered sugar
2 T. buttermilk
1½ t. vanilla extract

Beat butter and sugar at medium speed with an electric mixer until creamy. Add buttermilk; beat until spreading consistency. Stir in vanilla. Makes about ⅔ cup.

Sugar Cookie Pops

Buy several containers of colored sugars and jimmies so you'll have plenty for coating these cookie balls.

½ c. butter, softened
½ c. shortening
1 c. sugar
1 c. powdered sugar
2 eggs
¾ c. oil
2 t. vanilla extract
4 c. all-purpose flour
1 t. baking soda
1 t. salt
1 t. cream of tartar
colored sugars, sparkling sugars and
   multicolored jimmies
54 (4-inch) white craft sticks

Beat butter and shortening at medium speed with an electric mixer until fluffy; add sugars, beating well. Add eggs, oil and vanilla, beating until blended.

Combine flour and next 3 ingredients; add to butter mixture, blending well. Cover and chill dough 2 hours to overnight.

Shape dough into 1½-inch balls. Roll each ball in colored sugar or jimmies in individual bowls, pressing gently, if necessary, to coat balls. Place 2 inches apart on ungreased baking sheets. Insert craft sticks about 1 inch into each cookie to resemble a lollipop.

Bake at 350 degrees for 10 to 11 minutes, or until set. Let cool for 2 minutes on baking sheets; remove cookie pops to wire racks to cool completely. Makes 4½ dozen.

Sugar Cookie
Pops

Marshmallow Pops

10-oz. pkg. marshmallows
12 (4-inch) white craft sticks
12-oz. pkg. semi-sweet chocolate chips
2 T. shortening
Garnishes: candy sprinkles, toasted coconut,
  chopped nuts

Thread 2 marshmallows on each craft stick; set
aside. Melt chocolate chips and shortening in a
heavy saucepan over low heat, stirring constantly.
Dip marshmallows into chocolate mixture; sprinkle
with favorite garnish, if desired. Cool on wax
paper; store in refrigerator. Makes one dozen.

Marshmallow Pops

Marshmallow
Cookie Spiders

Marshmallow Cookie Spiders

Spooky but sweet, these spiders are easy to fix for school parties.

black licorice rope
4¼-oz. tube white icing
9-oz. pkg. chocolate-covered marshmallow cookies
16 assorted candies

For each spider, cut 4 pieces of licorice measuring 2 to 3 inches in length. Using a knife, cut each licorice piece in half lengthwise. Place each pair of legs opposite each other, flat-side down, on lightly greased wax paper. Cover inside ends of licorice with icing. Gently press cookie onto icing and legs. Use icing to "glue" the candies onto cookie for eyes. Allow icing to set up; carefully transfer cookie spiders to serving plates. Makes 8 spiders.

Message
Cookies

Message Cookies

*With alphabet cookie cutters, you can spell out
"Happy Halloween" or "Boo" for a tasty surprise!*

¾ c. butter, softened
1 c. powdered sugar
1 egg
1½ t. almond extract
4 c. all-purpose flour
⅛ t. salt
colored sprinkles

Beat butter and sugar at medium speed with an
electric mixer until creamy. Add egg and almond
extract; beat until smooth. Combine flour and salt
in a separate bowl; add to butter mixture, stirring
until a soft dough forms. Divide dough in half;
wrap in plastic wrap and chill one hour.

Roll dough to ¼-inch thickness on a lightly
floured surface. Use alphabet cookie cutters to cut
out your message; place the letters on greased
baking sheets. Bake at 350 degrees for 8 to 10
minutes; cool on wire racks with wax paper under-
neath racks. Spoon Icing over letters and top with
colored sprinkles. Makes 3 to 5 sets of cookies.

Icing:

¼ c. water
2 T. corn syrup
4 c. powdered sugar
1¼ t. almond extract
2 to 3 t. whipping cream

Combine water and corn syrup in a heavy saucepan. Add sugar, stirring until well blended; use a
pastry brush to scrape down any sugar on sides
of pan. Cook over low to medium heat until a
candy thermometer registers 100 degrees;
remove from heat.

Stir in almond extract and 2 teaspoons cream;
cool 5 minutes. Add enough remaining cream to
make desired consistency. Makes about one cup.

Simon the Centipede

8-oz. container frozen whipped topping, thawed
½ to 1 tsp. green food coloring
36 vanilla wafers
1 banana, peeled and cut into 36 slices
candy-coated chocolate mini-baking bits
cherry-flavored chewy fruit roll
6 spaghetti noodles, uncooked and broken in half
pull-and-peel red candy ropes, separated into
strands and divided
18 chocolate sandwich cookies, crumbled

Place whipped topping in a medium bowl; gently fold in food coloring.

Place one teaspoon whipped topping on the flat side of one vanilla wafer; top with a banana slice. Repeat with remaining whipped topping, vanilla wafers and banana slices. You'll have 36 stacks.

Put 6 stacks together in a row to make a log. Curve log slightly, if you'd like. Repeat with remaining stacks. Spread remaining whipped topping over each log. Cover and chill in the refrigerator at least 8 hours.

Attach chocolate baking bits to logs to resemble eyes and spots. Cut fruit roll into small pieces and attach to logs to resemble mouths. To make the antennae and legs: Cut red candy strands into 12 (7-inch) segments. Tie a loose knot into one candy strand, close to the end. Insert the tip of one spaghetti noodle into the knot and carefully tighten. Starting at the knot, wind the candy strand around the spaghetti, pressing gently as you go so the candy will stick to the spaghetti. Break the spaghetti off about an inch below the strand. Repeat with the remaining 11 (7-inch) segments of red candy strands and spaghetti. Insert into the logs just above the eyes to resemble antennae. Cut remaining red candy strands into 6 dozen (1-inch) segments and stick them into sides of logs to resemble legs. Serve on a bed of crumbled sandwich cookies. Serves 6.

NOTE
This cute dessert tastes a lot like banana pudding. The crisp vanilla wafers soften as it chills overnight, so it's perfect to eat with a spoon.

Simon the Centipede

Easy Marshmallows from Scratch

1½ c. water, divided
4 envs. unflavored gelatin
3 c. sugar
1¼ c. light corn syrup
¼ t. salt
2 t. vanilla extract
1½ c. powdered sugar, divided

Spray a 13"x9" baking pan with non-stick vegetable spray. Line with wax paper; coat wax paper with non-stick vegetable spray and set aside.

Pour ¾ cup water into a medium bowl and sprinkle gelatin over top; let stand for 5 minutes. Place sugar, corn syrup, remaining water, salt and vanilla in a heavy saucepan; bring to a boil. Cook over high heat for about 9 minutes, until mixture reaches the soft-ball stage, or 234 to 243 degrees on a candy thermometer. Beat hot mixture slowly into gelatin mixture for about 10 minutes, or until very stiff. Pour into prepared pan; smooth top with a spatula. Let stand overnight, uncovered, until firm.

Invert baking pan onto a surface covered with one cup powdered sugar; peel off wax paper. Cut into squares with a knife; roll in remaining powdered sugar to coat. Makes about 2 dozen.

Unbelievably easy to make... and perfect for outdoor parties. For marshmallows with different colors and flavors, add a small amount of unsweetened drink-mix powder to the mixture on the stove as you are heating it. Cut the marshmallows into shapes, if you wish, for floating in hot cocoa.

Easy Marshmallows from Scratch

Homemade Graham
Crackers

Homemade Graham Crackers

Include jumbo marshmallows and a dark chocolate bar for all the makings of gourmet s'mores.

1 c. butter, softened
½ c. dark brown sugar, packed
2 T. honey
2 t. vanilla extract
1½ c. all-purpose flour
1 c. whole-wheat pastry flour
2 t. cinnamon, divided
¾ t. baking soda
½ t. salt
3 T. sugar

Beat butter and next 3 ingredients at medium speed with an electric mixer for one minute, or until fluffy.

Combine flours, 1½ teaspoon cinnamon, baking soda and salt in a large bowl; add to butter mixture, beating just until blended.

Use dampened fingertips to press dough into a 17"x12" jelly-roll pan lined with parchment paper. Cover dough with additional parchment paper; smooth surface of dough with bottom of a dry measuring cup. Remove and discard top parchment paper. Combine remaining ½ teaspoon cinnamon and sugar in a small bowl; sprinkle over dough. Using tines of a fork, score dough into 24 squares, pressing completely through dough with each indentation.

Bake at 350 degrees for 20 minutes, or until golden and crisp. While crackers are still warm, score again. Cool completely in pan on a wire rack; break into individual crackers. Makes 2 dozen.

Double Chocolate-Covered Toffee Grahams

Adults will love these as much as kids do. They make a great gift for the hosts of a Halloween get-together and are perfect for making s'mores.

18 whole graham crackers, divided
6 (2-oz.) sqs. white melting chocolate, cut in half
4 (1-oz.) sqs. white baking chocolate, chopped
4 T. shortening, divided
6 (2-oz.) sqs. melting chocolate, cut in half
4 (1-oz.) sqs. semi-sweet baking chocolate, chopped
½ c. toffee baking bits

Break each graham cracker in half. Place white melting chocolate, white baking chocolate and 2 tablespoons shortening in a microwave-safe bowl. Microwave on high for one to 2 minutes, or until white chocolate is soft; stir until smooth. Dip 18 graham cracker squares entirely in melted white chocolate mixture. Place dipped grahams on a parchment paper-lined baking sheet. Chill for 20 minutes, or until white chocolate is firm. Dip the remaining graham crackers in a melted mixture of melting chocolate, semi-sweet chocolate and 2 tablespoons shortening. Drizzle any remaining semi-sweet chocolate and white chocolate over dipped grahams; sprinkle with toffee bits. Chill until firm. Makes 3 dozen.

Double Chocolate-Covered Toffee Grahams

Cappuccino Waffle Mix with
Coffee Syrup

Adults like treats too...so make some divine indulgences for grownup tastes for giving as hostess gifts or to trick-or-treating chaperones.

Cappuccino Waffle Mix with Coffee Syrup

Give this mix along with a jar of Coffee Syrup to the adults who ring your bell. They'll thank you for the eye-opener for breakfast after a night spent keeping up with the kids!

1⅓ c. all-purpose flour
⅓ c. powdered milk
⅓ c. powdered non-dairy creamer
2 t. baking powder
½ t. salt
2 T. instant coffee granules
½ t. cinnamon

Combine first 5 ingredients in a medium bowl. Combine coffee granules and cinnamon in a small bowl. Spoon half of flour mixture into a pint-size jar.

Layer coffee mixture over flour mixture. Spoon remaining flour mixture over coffee mixture. Seal container. Give with Coffee Syrup and attach instructions. Makes 2 cups.

Coffee Syrup:

1 c. brewed coffee
2 c. sugar

Combine both ingredients in a heavy saucepan; cook over medium-high heat, stirring constantly, until sugar dissolves. Bring to a boil, without stirring; boil 2 minutes. Remove from heat; cool to room temperature. Store in an airtight container in the refrigerator. Makes 1¾ cups.

Copy this tag for gift giving:

Cappuccino Waffle Mix

Beat ½ cup ½ softened butter, one cup sugar and 1½ teaspoons vanilla extract at medium speed with an electric mixer until creamy. Gradually blend butter mixture into waffle mix with a pastry blender or 2 forks until crumbly. Place mixture in a mixing bowl; add ¾ cup water and 2 eggs, stirring until just combined. Bake according to waffle iron manufacturer's directions. Serve with warm Coffee Syrup. Makes 5 to 6 waffles.

Wrap store-bought lollipops with white tissues secured with rubber bands. Draw black dots for eyes and a circle for a mouth to create howling ghost+ suckers. Arrange them in a pumpkin that's been hollowed out from the base. Drill small holes in the top and insert the sticks for a self-serve treat dispenser!

Harvest Moon
Lollipops

Harvest Moon Lollipops

These make a perfect party project for kids. (Younger children will need help inserting the lollipop sticks.) Arrange lollipops in a container filled with florist foam for an impressive centerpiece, or wrap individually in cellophane and give as party favors.

12 (10- to 12-inch) lollipop sticks
24-oz. pkg. chocolate-covered marshmallow sandwich pies
14-oz. pkg. orange candy melts
Garnish: Halloween candies, Halloween sugar cake decorations, decorator icing
Optional: ribbon

Insert one lollipop stick 2 to 3 inches into marshmallow center of each sandwich pie.

Microwave candy melts in a microwave-safe glass bowl on medium for one minute, or until melted, stirring once; spoon into a plastic zipping bag and seal.

Snip a small hole in one corner of the bag; pipe melted candy around where stick meets cookie to secure. Lay flat on wax paper; let stand until firm.

Pipe a border of melted candy around the cookies' edges. Use decorator icing to attach candies and/or cake decorations as desired. Tie ribbons around tops of sticks, if using. Makes one dozen.

Fairy Princess Wands

There's magic in the air when you serve these delicious treats. Make a wish and watch them disappear!

8 c. corn puff cereal
12-oz. pkg. white chocolate chips
½ c. light corn syrup
¼ c. butter or margarine
12 (12-inch) popsicle sticks
⅓ c. white chocolate chips
Optional: sugar sprinkles

Pour cereal into a large bowl and set aside. Combine white chocolate chips, corn syrup and butter in a microwave-safe bowl. Microwave on high for 2 minutes; stir until smooth. Drizzle white chocolate mixture over cereal, stirring to coat. Spoon mixture into a lightly greased 15"x10" jelly-roll pan. Spray your hands with cooking spray and press the mixture into an even layer. Let stand for 15 minutes.

Cut cereal mixture into stars with a 4-inch cookie cutter. Place stars on a wax paper-lined baking sheet. Cover and chill in the refrigerator for one hour or until firm. (Store leftover cereal mixture in an airtight container for snacking.)

To assemble the wands, insert a popsicle stick into each star. Place ⅓ cup white chocolate chips in a plastic zipping bag. Partially seal bag and set upright in a small microwave-safe measuring cup. Microwave on high for 20 to 30 seconds, or just until chips melt. Snip a tiny hole in one corner of bag to create a small opening. Drizzle melted chocolate over stars and decorate with sugar sprinkles, if desired. Let stand until firm. Store wands in an airtight container up to one week. Makes one dozen.

Fairy Princess Wands

Roasted Pumpkin Seeds

Roasted pumpkin seeds are an easy-to-make treat. Just rinse the seeds to remove any lingering pulp and dry well on paper towels. Toss them in a pan with a few tablespoons of melted butter and a sprinkle or two of salt then roast in a 350-degree oven for 15 minutes. Mmmmmm!

Cute Candy Apples

8 (4-inch) wooden craft sticks
8 Gala apples
2 (6½-oz.) pkgs. caramel apple wraps
16-oz. chocolate candy bar
16 ozs. white melting chocolate
orange gel paste
Garnish: colored sprinkles, chopped peanuts,
    black decorating gel

Insert craft sticks into apples. Cover each apple
with one caramel wrap. Microwave in a microwave-safe dish on high for 15 to 20 seconds. Cool.

Melt chocolate bar in a small saucepan over low
heat. Dip each apple into chocolate; let excess drip
off. Cool on buttered wax paper until set.

Melt white melting chocolate in a small saucepan
over low heat; stir in orange food coloring.

Dip or drizzle each apple with white chocolate
mixture; let excess drip off. Decorate with desired
toppings. Cool on buttered wax paper until set.
Makes 8 apples.

Cute Candy
Apples

White Meringue
Ghosts

White Meringue Ghosts

6 egg whites
½ tsp. cream of tartar
¾ c. sugar
½ tsp. almond extract
1 T. mini semi-sweet chocolate chips
string licorice

Beat egg whites and cream of tartar at high speed
with an electric mixer until foamy. Gradually add
sugar, 1 tablespoon at a time, beating until stiff
peaks form and sugar dissolves (2 to 4 minutes).
Add extract; beat until blended.

Spoon mixture into a plastic zipping bag; snip
a small hole in one corner, and pipe mixture into
ghostly shapes on parchment paper-lined baking
sheets. Add chocolate chips for eyes. If desired,
cut licorice into 2-inch pieces. Firmly pinch ends
together. Insert 1 in top of each ghost for a hanger.

Bake at 200 degrees for 2 hours. Turn oven off,
and let meringues stand in closed oven with light
on for 8 hours. Makes 16 meringues.

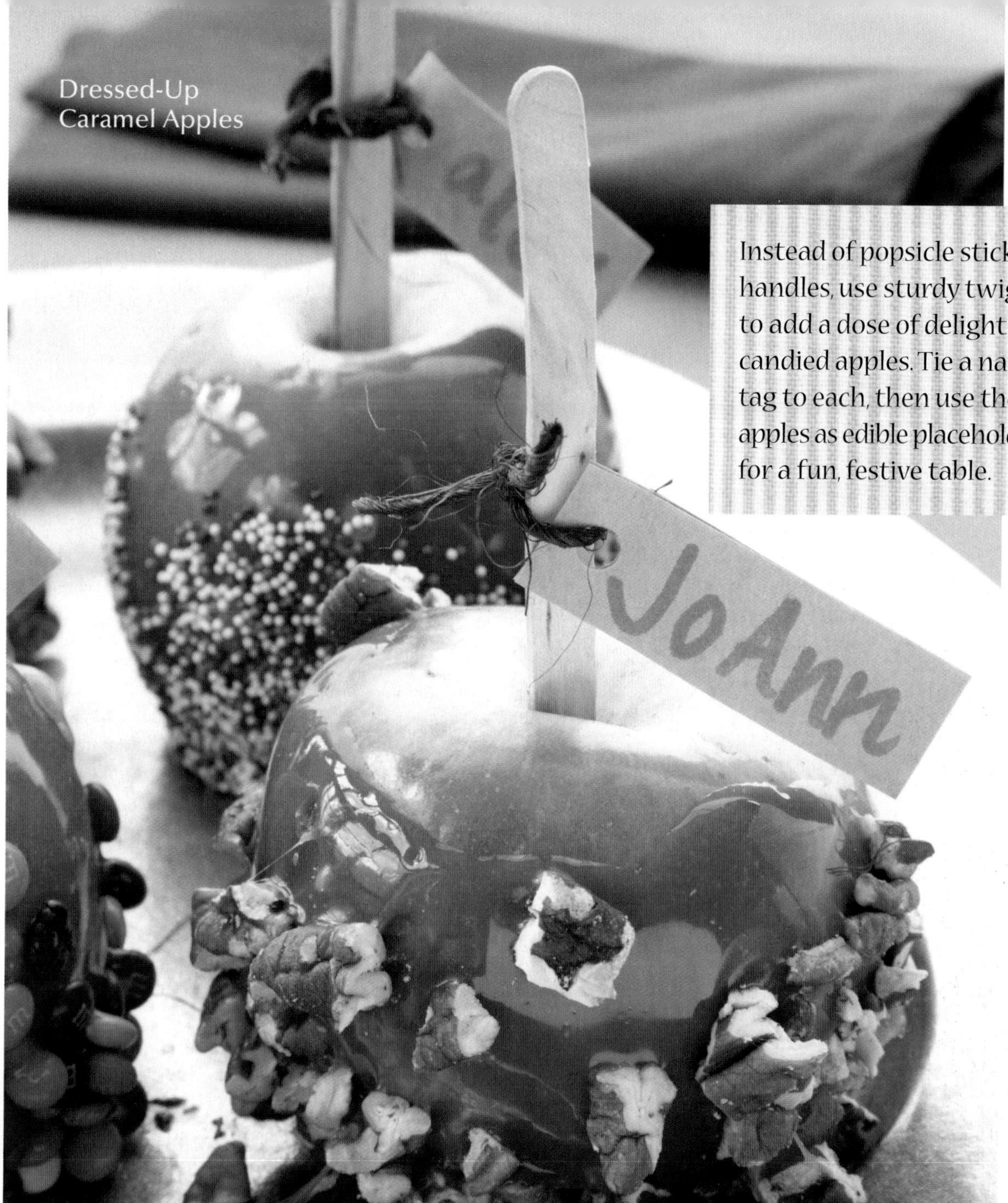

Dressed-Up
Caramel Apples

Instead of popsicle stick handles, use sturdy twigs to add a dose of delight to candied apples. Tie a name tag to each, then use the apples as edible placeholders for a fun, festive table.

Dressed-Up Caramel Apples

6 apples
6 (4-inch) wooden craft sticks or twigs
14-oz. pkg. caramels, unwrapped
2 T. water
Garnishes: chopped nuts, multi-colored sprinkles, candy-coated chocolate mini-baking bits

Wash and dry apples; insert sticks into stem end of apples and set aside. Combine caramels and water in a saucepan. Cook and stir over medium-low heat until caramels are completely melted. Dip apples into melted caramel until well coated; let excess drip off. Dip bottoms of apples into desired garnish. Set apples on a plate lined with buttered wax paper. Chill for at least one hour. Makes 6.

Candy Corn
Popcorn Balls
(page 95)

Chocolate
Spiderweb Treats

Chocolate Spiderweb Treats

4 c. mini marshmallows, packed
⅓ c. creamy peanut butter
2 T. butter or margarine
6 c. chocolate crispy rice cereal
12-oz. pkg. milk chocolate chips
½ c. white chocolate chips

Combine marshmallows, peanut butter and butter in a large microwave-safe bowl. Microwave on high for 2 minutes. Stir peanut butter mixture vigorously with a wooden spoon until smooth. Add cereal and stir until well coated. Quickly spoon mixture into a lightly greased 15"x10" jelly-roll pan and press into an even layer. Cool for 5 minutes, or until firm.

Cut cereal mixture into circles with a 3-inch round cookie cutter.

Place milk chocolate chips in a small microwave-safe bowl. Microwave on medium for 2 minutes, or until chocolate is just beginning to melt. Stir chocolate until smooth.

Place white chocolate chips in a plastic zipping bag. Partially seal bag and set upright in a small microwave-safe measuring cup. Microwave on medium for one minute. Gently squeeze bag until chocolate is smooth. Snip a tiny hole in one corner of bag to create a small opening.

Spread melted milk chocolate over top of one circle. While milk chocolate is still soft, drizzle white chocolate in 3 rings on top of milk chocolate. Starting at the center, pull a toothpick through the rings to create a "web." Repeat with remaining circles and chocolate. Refrigerate for 30 minutes, or until chocolate is firm. Store Chocolate Spiderweb Treats in an airtight container up to 3 days. Makes 1½ dozen.

Chocolate-Dipped Spoons

Stir a little sweetness into mugs of steaming drinks like cocoa or coffee.

12-oz. pkg. semi-sweet chocolate chips
2 t. shortening
35 to 45 plastic spoons
Garnish: candies for decorating

Line baking sheets with parchment paper; set aside. Place chocolate chips in a microwave-safe bowl; microwave on medium for 2 minutes, or until melted, stirring every 30 seconds. Add shortening to thin the chocolate; stir gently. Dip each plastic spoon into chocolate mixture to cover the bowl of the spoon; place on parchment paper to set. Arrange candies on spoons as desired while chocolate is still soft; let cool completely. Makes 35 to 45 spoons.

Chocolate-Dipped Spoons

fiendish fun

ALL DRESSED UP with places to go. Halloween demands fun disguises. Sometimes a simple mask or painted face does the trick, and other times only a costume will do.

[*Pixie, kobold, elf, and sprite.*
All are on their rounds tonight . . .]
—JOEL BENTON

Birds of a Feather

If donning a full-length costume isn't your cup of tea, make an embellished mask to wear with street clothes for a bit of mystery. The tools of haberdashery are perfect for making masks. Get carried away with little odds and ends and sewing notions like feathers, lace, faux petals and leaves, sequins and ribbon.

MATERIALS

plain masks
spray paint
paintbrush
craft or hot glue
variety of feathers
large sequins
spray glitter or sprinkle glitter
ribbon

Natural feathers adorn this simple mask reminiscent of hawk wings.

FEATHER MASK

- **Spray** paint the mask brown.
- **Brush** the bottom third of the back side, or concave side, of each feather with craft glue and arrange in overlapping rows from the outside of the mask toward the nose to create a fanlike effect.
- **Replace** elastic band with ribbon cut to fit.

ORANGE MASK

- **Secure** the sequins in an overlapping spiral fashion with hot glue.
- **Hot glue** a bright feather to one side as an accent.
- **Replace** elastic band with ribbon cut to fit.

Large orange sequins give this mask a Jack-o'-Lantern glow. A fluffy orange feather adds fireworks.

Spray glitter makes this mask come together quickly. Two raven feathers at the edge of each eye look like long fluttering lashes.

WHITE MASK

- **Spray** mask with glitter glue and let dry.
- **Hot glue** a black feather to the outer edge of each eye.
- **Replace** elastic band with ribbon cut to fit.

Painted Faces

A bit of face paint and imagination is all that's required to transform children into creatures and critters and cute things…oh my! Have older kids man the face-painting booth. It will become the main attraction of any party for the younger set.

Look for non-toxic, hypo-allergenic face paints that are soap-and-water washable to avoid surprises like stained clothes or allergic reactions.

PRECIOUS PUMPKIN

Doe eyes stare from this little one's glowing Jack-o'-Lantern face made from three face-paint colors: orange, yellow and black.

- **Outline** the face with orange paint and fill in with evenly spaced vertical lines in contrasting yellow and orange to create the ribbed skin of a plump pumpkin.
- **Frame** the eyes with black triangles.
- **Outline** then fill in the lips for a finished look.

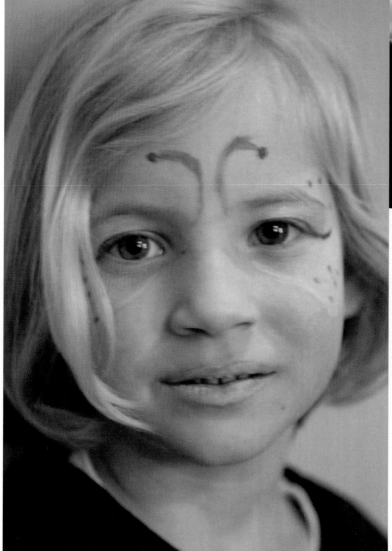

FLUTTERING BUTTERFLY

Pastel princesses are delightful, but this delicate butterfly is equally enchanting. Pair it with a gossamer gown from the dress-up trunk for a complete costume.

- **Paint** wings to extend beyond each eye, then fill in with chartreuse and purple accents.
- **Complete** the look with curved antennae and painted lips.

AHOY, MATEY!

Ready to collect a night's worth of booty, this scruffy fellow is easy to treasure.

- **Blacken** one eye with paint to create an eye patch.
- **Paint** the outline of a knotted scarf and fill in with strokes of red.
- **A sea sponge** just dabbed in black paint then lightly blotted on the chin creates the believable after-five shadow.

PURRRRFECTLY PRETTY

All the markings of a pink panther, but so easy to create. Use a trio of pink, black and white face paint.

- **Paint** slanted triangles above the brow pink. Color the eyelids and base of the nose pink, too.
- **Paint** the chin and above the top lip white.
- **Add** black accents around the eyes, on the tip of the nose and above the lip.
- **Finish** with thin strokes for whiskers. Meow!

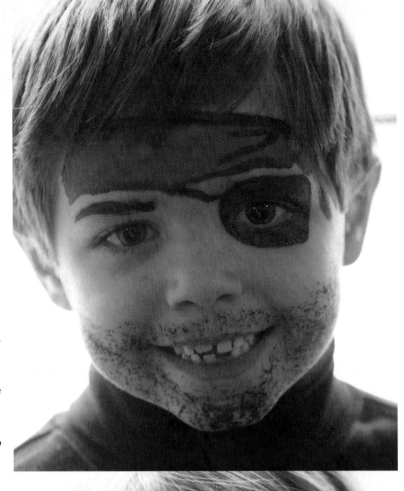

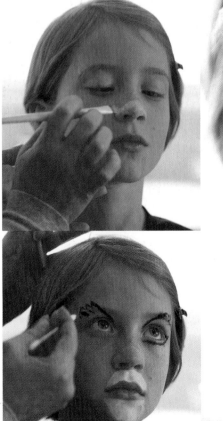

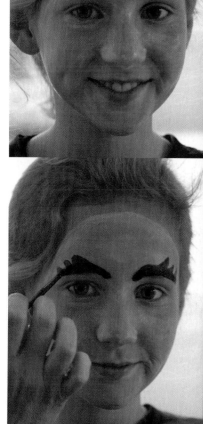

WICKEDLY WITCHY

Add a broom and a pointy hat to top things off, and this little pretty has a fitting costume for fright night. A green face lends a sickly pallor and black highlights take the look to haunting heights.

- **Paint** the entire face green.
- **Add** black triangles to the forehead, cheeks and brow.
- **Carefully rim** the eyes in black and add lines for wrinkles.
- **Fill in** lips and add a black line for a cleft on the chin.

Unique Costumes

Even if you're short on time, you can "treat" your child to a unique Halloween costume. Choose from a funny bug, a plump tomato, a fancy fairy and a ferociously friendly lion, as seen on the following pages. Instructions for the tomato, bug, fairy and lion costumes are on pages 192-196.

FANCY FAIRY
The fluttering fairy is sure to elicit smiles on trick-or-treat night and be a favorite from the dress-up trunk all year long. Find the how-to on page 196.

FEROCIOUSLY FRIENDLY LION
There's nothing cowardly about this lion! Turn a plain brown sweat suit into an adorable costume for a fall carnival...or just for playtime. See instructions on page 195.

Fun and Games

Halloween is about more than howls and haunting, it's a perfect time to gather together...adults and kids alike...to share a meal, make some crafts, and play silly games. Enjoy a crisp October evening in the yard bobbing for apples or doughnuts, playing hide-and-seek or becoming the master of the beanbag toss.

TREAT BUCKET

Instead of using the same old pillowcase or plastic pumpkin to carry candy, kids can have fun creating their own treat pails.

MATERIALS

colorful plastic pails
paint pens or permanent markers
stickers, glitter glue and other
   decorative items
glue or double-stick tape

• **Choose** a pail relative to the size of the child so he or she won't be weighed down while walking the neighborhood.

• **Write** the child's name with paint pen or permanent marker on the outside of the pail before the decorating begins.

• **Let kids get creative** with stickers, glitter glue, ribbon and other finds to decorate their pails. Glow-in-the-dark paint and stickers are great for visibility on Halloween night.

TIP

Make sure the paint has dried before kids handle the pails. A hair dryer set on medium heat speeds up the process. Paint pen can be cleaned off most surfaces with non-acetone fingernail polish remover. For permanent marker, try rubbing alcohol.

Beanbag Toss

This DIY beanbag toss is a fun game for kids to play at any Halloween event. Find the instructions for the bags below and the pumpkin cutout on the facing page.

MATERIALS

plywood board
pencil
pushpin
short length of string
drill
jigsaw tool
sandpaper
small piece of wood
small hinge
short piece of chain
paint
paintbrushes
detail brushes
12 handheld beanbags

TIME TO TOSS

If you're feeling extra crafty, make the beanbags for tossing. Simply sew together 2 pieces of Halloween fabric, facing wrong-side out, until almost closed. Turn the fabric right-side out, fill with dry beans at the opening and then sew it closed. Repeat so you have 3 or more beanbags.

PUMPKIN CUTOUT

Making the cutout for the beanbag toss can be a fun family activity. Fold it up and store it for use year after year.

• **Using** ¼-inch or ½-inch plywood, draw desired shape. Use a pushpin and a short length of string to guide your pencil to outline an even circle.

• **Give** your pumpkin a face by outlining the shape of the pumpkin's eyes and mouth with a pencil. Make sure to draw the edges of the openings large enough for a beanbag to easily pass through.

• **Using** a power drill, drill holes in the corners and around the edges of openings to make them easier to cut. Using a jigsaw, cut out the outlines of the eyes and mouth.

• **Use** a coarse sandpaper block to sand around all of the edges to prevent splinters or cuts.

• **Attach** a small piece of wood to the back for the stand. Use a small hinge to fasten the board onto the back of the pumpkin. Use a short piece of chain with small hooks to link the base of the pumpkin to the base of the stand, which will stabilize the wood cutout.

• **Prime** then paint the cutout orange. Trim the edges of the eyes, nose, mouth and pumpkin top with black paint. Remember not to move your pumpkin until the paint is completely dry.

CHAPTER 6

quick tricks

WHEN TIME IS TICKING and guests will soon ring the bell, look to these displays, treats and crafts for ideas that will wow your friends and family yet are oh-so easy to do!

Mini Cupcake Pumpkin

Candy Corn Trifles

MINI CUPCAKE PUMPKIN

Arrange 2 dozen store-bought mini cupcakes in the shape of a pumpkin, using 2 for the stem. Frost the body of the pumpkin with orange-tinted canned white frosting, leaving the eyes, nose and mouth unfrosted. Use green-tinted canned frosting for the stem. Add shimmering sprinkles to the stem, eyes, nose and mouth.

CANDY CORN TRIFLES

Layer store-bought angel food cake, prepared vanilla pudding tinted orange with food coloring, and lemon gelatin.

Tombstone
Cookies

Baby Ghosts

Gingerbread
Mummies

BABY GHOSTS

Microwave 12 ounces of white chocolate in a microwave-safe bowl on high 60 seconds, stirring every 15 seconds, until smooth. For each ghost, dip three-quarters of a peanut-shaped peanut butter cookie in the melted chocolate. Top with 2 mini chocolate chips for eyes. Place prepared ghosts on wax paper and refrigerate to set.

GINGERBREAD MUMMIES

Arrange gingerbread men on wax paper and place 2 semi-sweet chocolate chips where eyes should be. With a large leaf piping tip, pipe ribbons of white decorating icing back and forth over the cookie, completely covering it to resemble gauze, but letting the chocolate chip eyes peek out.

TOMBSTONE COOKIES

Arrange a variety of cookies on wax paper (we used half-dipped fudge grahams, vanilla sandwich fingers, and black and white Milan-style sandwich cookies) and pipe the letters RIP in orange, green or black decorating icing using a #3 or #4 round tip.

Peanut Masks

Skinned Knees

PEANUT MASKS

Embellish peanut-shaped peanut butter cookies with two small circles of decorator's icing in orange or green. Top with 2 chocolate-covered raisins for pupils.

SKINNED KNEES

Press prepared snickerdoodle dough in the center with the back of a spoon to create a concave cavity. Fill with a spoonful of strawberry jam. Bake according to package directions.

Tire Tracks

TIRE TRACKS

Take one fudge-striped cookie and place upside-down on a microwave-safe plate. Top with red icing, 6 mini marshmallows and a sprinkle of toasted coconut. Microwave on high 15 seconds or until marshmallows begin to puff. Top with a second cookie and smash down. Fill in the lines on top of the cookie with chocolate frosting to make 2" tire tracks.

SCARY SPIDERS

Place one chocolate-covered marshmallow sandwich cookie upside down. Top with black decorating icing. Cut 2 black licorice twists in half lengthwise and then in half crosswise to make 8 thin legs. Press one end of each leg into the black icing. Top with a second cookie. Affix 2 jellybean eyes with black icing.

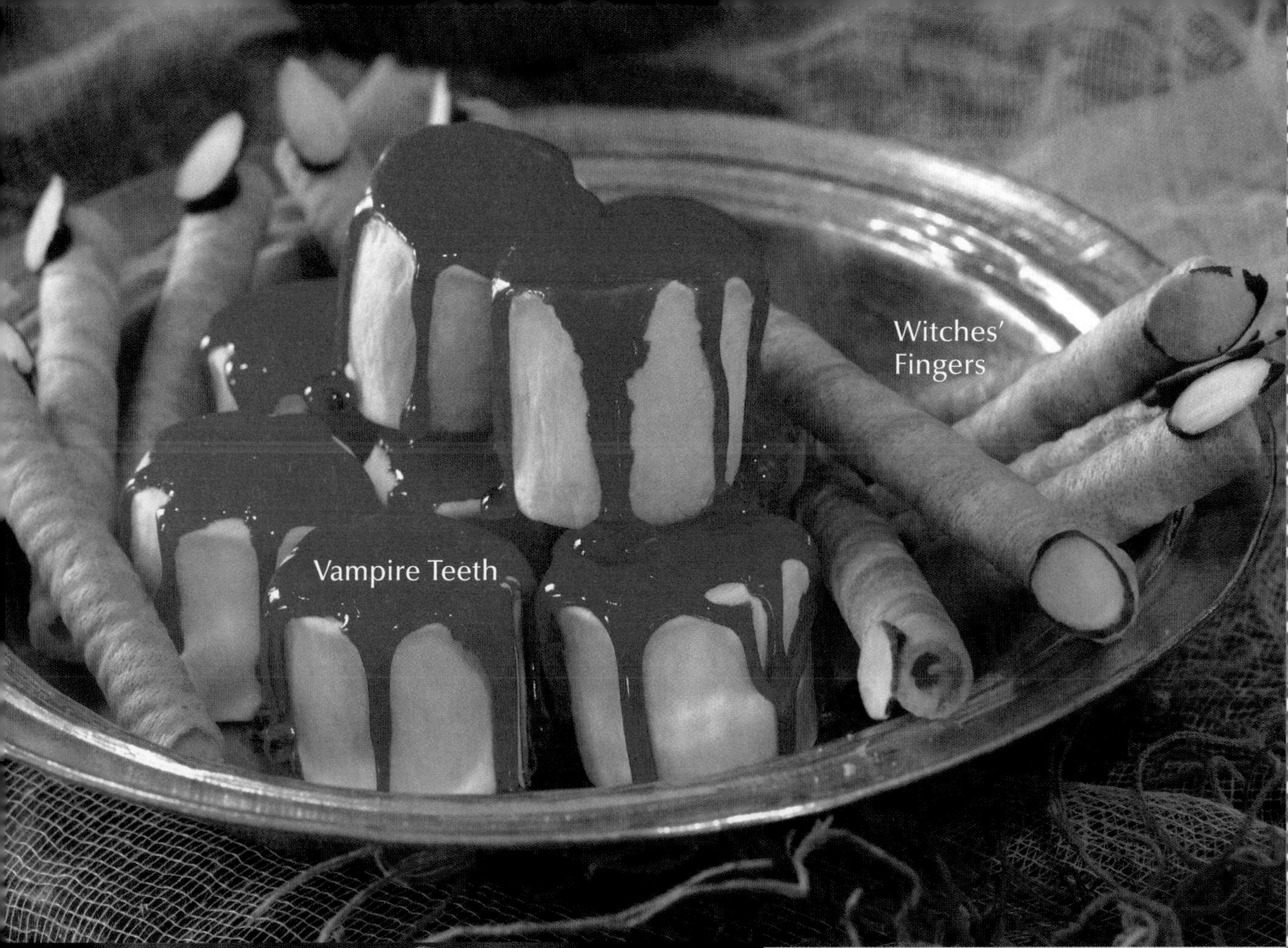

Witches'
Fingers

Vampire Teeth

Scary Spiders

VAMPIRE TEETH
Place 10 large marshmallows on
wax paper. Unwrap 10 red-cherry
hard candies and place in a small
microwave-safe bowl. Microwave on
high 30 seconds or until molten and
bubbling. Immediately pour syrup
over marshmallows, dividing evenly.
Reheat candy as needed, microwav-
ing 10 seconds to re-melt.

WITCHES' FINGERS
Cut 10 cream-filled chocolate wafer
sticks in half. Affix a sliced almond to
one end of each with white frosting.

Wizard Hats

WIZARD HATS

Place 6 (2-oz.) squares melting chocolate in a 2-cup glass measure. Microwave on high 2 minutes, stirring every 30 seconds. Dip sugar cones in the melted chocolate, tilting the measuring glass to coat. Place, pointy end up, on top of large chocolate-covered marshmallow moon pies. Pipe icing around the area where the cone and moon pies meet. Press nonpareils and other candies into icing to create a hatband.

Haunted Houses

Haunted Houses can be made entirely of ready-made cookies and candies and cobbled together in inventive ways using canned frosting. A haunted farmhouse sits next to a yummy candy pumpkin patch. An embellished abode inspired by the witch's house from Hansel & Gretel is flanked by a graveyard with a resident ghost (on following page). Making these frightfully fun houses is a great party activity or Halloween tradition to start with your family!

PUMPKIN PATCH HOUSE

house – chocolate-covered peanut butter
    wafer bars
mortar – canned chocolate frosting
roof – chocolate graham crackers
roof tiles – chocolate candy corn pieces
roof decoration: purple candy-coated chocolates
door – chocolate graham cracker
door knob – purple candy-coated chocolate
grass – green-tinted canned white frosting and
    dyed green coconut
dirt – canned chocolate frosting
fence – pretzel sticks and orange marshmallow
    ghosts
gate – half-dipped fudge grahams
garden – gummy worms, candy pumpkins and
    candy corn

Graveyard House

GRAVEYARD HOUSE

house – chocolate-covered peanut butter wafer bars

mortar – canned chocolate frosting

roof – chocolate graham crackers

roof tiles – chocolate sandwich cookie thin crisps
   (from 100-calorie snack packs)

roof decoration – orange and black sprinkles and candy corn

house decoration – orange chocolate-covered candies

windows – half-dipped fudge grahams

window panes – orange-tinted canned white frosting

door – any rectangular white cookie

stepping stones – mini golden sandwich cookies

grass – green-tinted canned white frosting and dyed green coconut

dirt – canned chocolate frosting

tombstones – Tombstone Cookies (page 165)

cemetery – swirled chocolate chips and marshmallow ghost

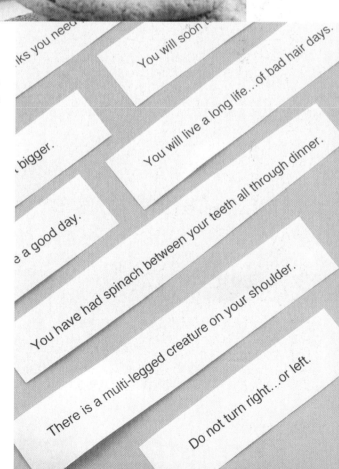

COOKIE JAR

An empty pickle jar can quickly be reinvented as a Halloween-inspired treat jar with eyes to catch the cookie thief. By using removable window decals (see resources on page 201) and a grosgrain ribbon embellishment on the lid, the jar can be easily recycled to fit a different seasonal theme.

MISFORTUNES

Want to add some humor to your cookie swap or Halloween party? Get personal! Come up with silly "misfortunes" geared to your guests and print them out on letter-size paper. Cut your messages into narrow strips and insert them into store-bought fortune cookies.

TREAT BAGS

These cute bags are anything but ordinary and can be used for candy, cookies, party favors or gifts for the host or hostess. Purchase paper gift sacks in a range of complementary hues. Trace Halloween shapes (see stencils on page 197) on patterned scrapbook paper and cut them out. Use hot glue to secure the shapes to the front of the bags for a dimensional effect. Fill the bags with the desired goodies and fold the top edge over. Punch 2 holes, about ½-inch apart, through the folded edge. Lace ribbon through the holes and tie in a bow or knot to secure. Abracadabra!

ICING CONE GOODIE BAGS

Pick up clear plastic icing bags from your kitchen store or baker's supply. The conical shape makes them ideal for creating giant "candy corn" favors. Chocolate-covered peanut butter pieces and chocolate-covered candies in Halloween hues are layered to replicate candy corn-stripes. A galvanized bucket becomes a self-serve dispenser with a removable-decal greeting.

CRITTER JAR

Create creepy, crawly specimen jars with dried moss, sticks from your yard, rocks and plastic "critters" of the eight-legged kind. Build your display on inverted jar lids. A glue gun secures items in the scene. When the stage is set, carefully set the jar over the display and twist to close. Arrange several on a web-covered tray accented with a few escapees!

TIN CAN MUMMY VASES

Raid your recycling bin, medicine cabinet and yard to make this quick and easy arrangement. Wash empty tin cans and remove the labels if you wish. With a glue gun, secure a cotton ball to the center of the can to create the bump of a nose. Wrap the cans with several layers of gauze bandaging and secure the end with more glue. Glue craft eyes above the nose. Gather a bouquet of dried flowers or seedpods from your yard and give them a very light misting of black spray paint. Arrange them in the vase to create a frightful mummy hairdo!

PAPER LANTERNS

A black cat's silhouette (see page 185) and bold "boo" in black stand out on pale parchment paper globes. Find plain white paper lanterns at party supply stores. Draw or trace your desired message or shape on the lantern very carefully without puncturing. Use a foam brush and acrylic paint to fill in your design. It will dry and be ready for hanging in a matter of minutes.

VELLUM VOTIVES

Paper lunch bags are transformed to emit a howling glow. Cut freeform circles (or use the stencils on page 184) for eyes and mouth on both sides of the bag. A few long slits in each side will allow illumination on all sides. Secure sheets of frosted vellum behind the cutouts using gift tape. Fill the bags with gravel or sand to stabilize. As a precaution, use battery-powered votives for a worry-free glow.

gooseberry grab bag

A TREASURE TROVE of stencils and patterns.

[*The secret to creativity is knowing how to hide your sources.*]
—ALBERT EINSTEIN

Ghost Stencil

Frankenstein Stencil

Bat Stencil
(shown on page 18)

Ghost Face Stencil
(shown page 18)

Cat Stencil
(similar to page 19 and page 176)

Witch Stencil
(similar to page 18)

Spiderweb Stencil
(shown on page 19)

"Boo" Welcome Mat
(shown on page 37)

Come on by
for Halloween
We promise you
will
DIG
the scene.

PARTY

Date . . . .

Time . . . .

Place . . . .

. . . .

Given by . . . .

Be there ... or ELSe.

Gravedigger Invitation

CALLING ALL ★ SPOOKY CATS:

Pull on your whiskers
this Halloween
for a spooky cat party
like you've never seen!
★
WEAR A CAT COSTUME
TO MY HOUSE ON

_____

at _____ o'clock

PLACE _____

GIVEN
BY _____

ME
OW.

Spooky Cat Invitation

EMBALMING FLUID

Label for Soap Bubbles

THE
VELVET
DEVIL

MERLOT
2007
WASHINGTON STATE

Printable Wine Labels

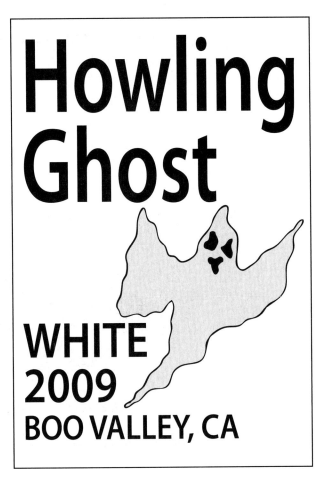

Howling
Ghost

WHITE
2009
BOO VALLEY, CA

Printable Soda Pop Labels

Bug Costume
(shown on page 156)

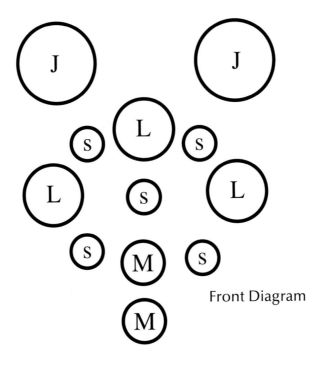

Front Diagram

• **Enlarge** the wing pattern on page 193 on a photocopier to desired size…if necessary, cut the pattern apart and enlarge by sections, then tape enlarged copies together. Using enlarged pattern, cut wings, then 2 jumbo spots, 3 large spots, 2 medium spots and 5 small spots from felt for wings; cut 2 jumbo spots, 4 large spots, 4 medium spots and 10 small spots from felt for spots on wings. Cut stripe from remaining felt color.

• **Glue** the spots, stripe and hook and loop fastener on the wings referring to the wing pattern for placement. Glue the spots on the front of the romper using the front diagram for reference.

• **Measure** length of romper sleeve from under arm to end of cuff; add 3½" for each "extra" arm. Measure height of cuff; add 1". Cut a rectangle of fabric the determined measurements; use fusible tape to hem one short edge. Fuse a length of tape along one long edge on the right side of the fabric piece; remove the paper backing. Matching right sides, fuse long edges together; turn right-side out. Fold raw end up 1½" two times to make a cuff. Fill the toe of one sock with fiberfill. Insert the sock in the cuff end of the arm and glue to secure. Lightly stuff the arm and glue the opening closed.

• **Use** safety pins to secure the arms to the romper from the inside. The arms should be close together. To make the arms move together, sew a length of heavy-duty thread between each arm…make sure it's long enough for the arms to hang slightly.

• **Make** the mittens by turning a sock wrong-side out. Cut a slit in the toe long and wide enough for the child's thumb. Use glue to "seam" the edges together, then allow to dry. Turn mitten right-side out.

• **Create** antennae by inserting a pipe cleaner in each spring of headband; trim even with end of spring. Wrap the remainder of pipe cleaners around springs. Glue a pom-pom to the end of each antenna.

Wing Pattern

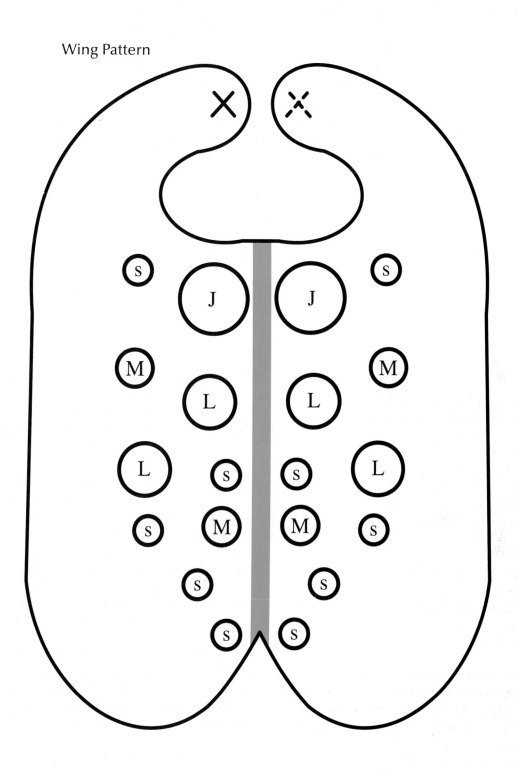

Tomato Costume
(shown on page 156)

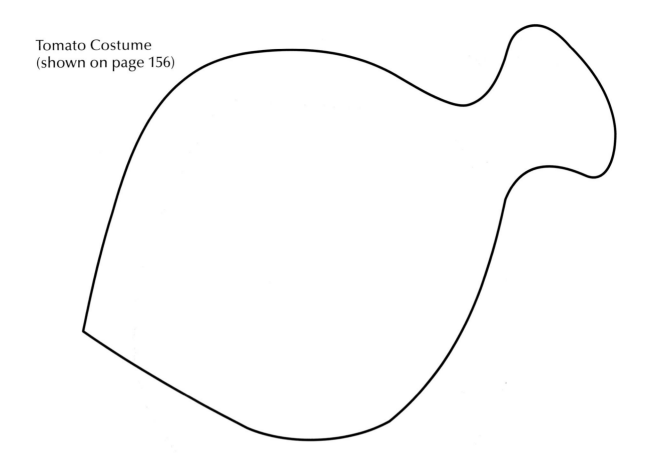

MATERIALS:
3 pieces of red felt and 1 piece of green felt for body, stem
    and leaf
scissors and pinking shears
ribbon
needle and thread
¾" width elastic
safety pins
stuffing: polyester fiberfill, plastic bags or foam peanuts
tracing paper
pipe cleaner
fabric or craft glue

• **Place** the red felt pieces together and fold in half (when folded the fabric should reach from elbow to elbow and hang from the shoulder to 3 inches below the child's knees). Use a dinner plate centered on the fold to mark a half-circle for the head opening and cut out.
• **Place** the felt pieces over the child's head. Tie a piece of ribbon around each shoulder to gather the felt…it's okay to tie the ribbon at the top of the shoulders because it will be on the inside when you're finished.
• **Mark** the armholes on each side of the costume

and then take it off the child. Sew up the sides… only sew up to the marks and sew through all four layers of felt! Sew the felt layers together around the bottom edge. For the elastic casing, fold the bottom edge up 1½ inches and pin in place. Leaving an opening to insert the elastic, sew along the casing edge.
• **Turn** the costume right-side out and place it back on the child. Insert the elastic in the casing and adjust to desired tightness and height around the legs. Trim the elastic and secure with a safety pin. Working through the armholes, stuff the tomato to desired plumpness.
• **Trace** the leaf pattern above onto tracing paper. Using pinking shears, cut out 5 leaves and one 3½" diameter circle from the green felt…you will also need to cut a 6"x12" rectangle for the stem and a 1"x30" strip for the ties. Glue the circle at the center of the tie strip. Glue a 6" length of pipe cleaner along one long edge of the stem felt piece.
• **Roll** the felt around the pipe cleaner, then glue to secure. Glue one end of the stem to the center of the circle on the side with the tie strip. Pinching the leaf at the narrow section and gluing the pinched area to the circle, glue the leaves around the stem; bend the stem slightly.

Lion Costume
(shown on page 157)

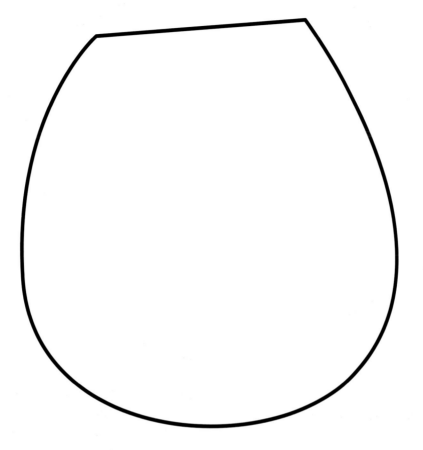

MATERIALS:

plain brown sweat suit

tracing paper

scissors

brown felt

glue

plastic headband

yarn

hook and loop fasteners

beige felt

cardboard

fiberfill

safety pins

• **Trace** the ear pattern above onto tracing paper; use the pattern to cut two ears from brown felt. Glue the ears to a plastic headband. Gluing as you go, make 8" long loops of yarn along the headband for the mane.

• **Measure** around the child's neck and add 2" then cut a strip of felt 1" wide by the determined measurement to create the collar. Apply self-adhesive hook and loop fasteners at opposite sides of the ends of the strips. Working on the same side of the strip with the rough piece of fastener, glue 8" long loops of yarn along the strip. Repeat to make wristbands.

• **Cut** a 7"x23" piece of beige felt for the tail. Glue the long edges together to form a tube; turn right-side out. Wrap yarn around a 5" square piece of cardboard…wrap lots of yarn for a fuller tail. Tightly knot a length of yarn around the yarn at one end of the cardboard; cut the yarn at opposite end. Tie a length of yarn around tassel near top.

• **Glue** top of tassel inside one end of tail. Stuff tail with fiberfill and pin to pants. Glue an oval of beige felt to the front of the shirt.

Fairy Costume
(shown on page 157)

Running Stitches

Making A Fabric Circle

• **Measure** the child from the back of the neck to the wrist for the capelet; double the measurement. Cut a square of fabric with pinking shears to the determined measurement.

• **Determine** inside cutting line measurement by measuring around child's head; divide measurement by 4. Using determined measurement for inside cutting line and original neck to wrist measurement for outside cutting line, follow **Making A Fabric Circle** (above) to cut out capelet.

• **Pin** desired number of photocopies of the circle design, 2½" from the outer edge and spacing evenly, to wrong side of the capelet...the design should show through to the right side. Using dimensional paint and working on the right side of the capelet, randomly draw stars in the upper area of the capelet; press an acrylic jewel in the center of each star. Make dots of paint over each circle design, then draw short, wavy lines along the outer edge.

• **Make** the collar by cutting a 3"x24" strip of fabric. Use dimensional paint to draw wavy lines and stars along one long edge; attach one jewel to the center of each star. Using ribbon, work **Running Stitches** (above) along opposite edge.

• **Cut** an 18" square from fabric. Using 9" as the outer cutting line and no inner cutting line, follow **Making A Fabric Circle** (above) to cut out hat piece. Use dimensional paint to draw wavy lines along edge and random stars on hat. Using elastic thread, work Running Stitches 2" in from edge. Gather hat to fit head and knot ends on inside of hat.

• **Make** antennae by coiling one end of each pipe cleaner and glue to headband; wrap ends around finger to curl. Brush headband and antenna with gold glitter paint.

Treat Bag Embellishments
(shown on page 172)

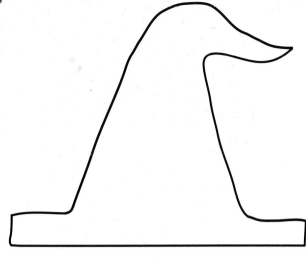

Witch's Hat

Pumpkin

Wrapped Candy

OCTOBER

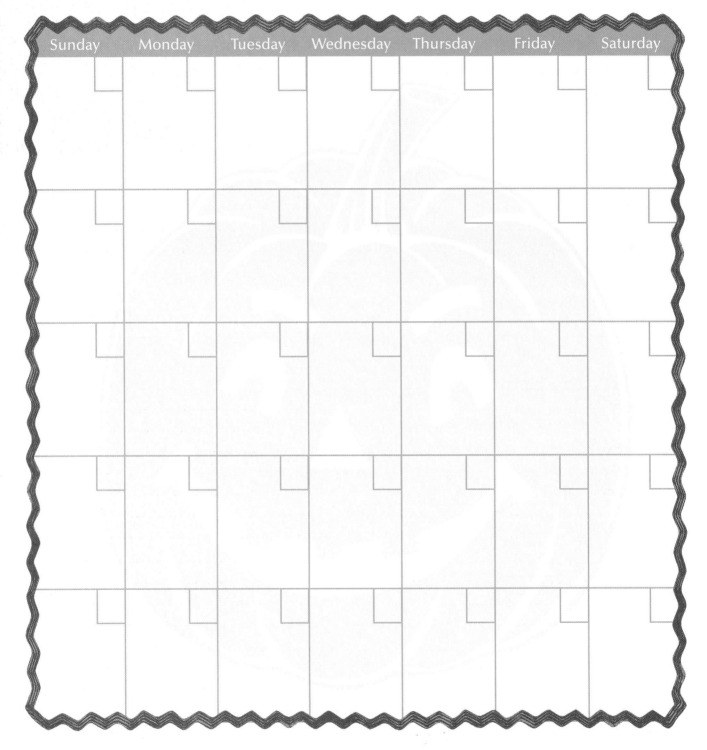

Sunday	Monday	Tuesday	Wednesday	Thursday	Friday	Saturday

Halloween Decorating Planner

List what you'll need for Halloween decorations through the house.

Decorative materials needed

from the yard ....
....

from around the house..
....

from the store..
....

other...

Halloween decorations

for the table ....
....

for the door ....
....

for the porch ....
....

for the yard...
....

other...
....
....
....
....
....
....
....
....

Halloween Memories

Capture highlights of this year's best Halloween moments here.

Treasured Traditions

Record your family's favorite Halloween customs and pastimes

....
....
....
....
....
....
....
....
....
....
....
....

Special Halloween Activities

Keep a list of events you look forward to year after year

....
....
....
....
....
....
....
....
....
....
....
....
....
....

Party Guest List

Pantry List

Party To-Do List

Resources

www.americanfolklore.net For age-appropriate ghost stories from each state in the Union.

www.myluckyfortune.com For plain and Halloween-colored fortune cookies.

www.orientaltrading.com For treat bag novelties and candy.

www.michaels.com For craft supplies, pumpkin carving tools, paint and embellishments.

www.hobbylobby.com For face paints and accessories; feathers, sequins, glitter for masks.

www.dickblick.com For plain masquerade masks.

www.nostalgicsweets.com For hard-to-find classic candy.

www.worldmarket.com For paper lanterns and novelties.

www.joann.com For fabric and trimmings.

Our Story

BACK IN 1984, we were next-door neighbors raising our families in the little town of Delaware, Ohio. We were two moms with small children looking for a way to do what we loved and stay home with the kids too. We shared a love of home cooking and making memories with family & friends. After many a conversation over the backyard fence, Gooseberry Patch was born.

We put together the first catalog & cookbooks at our kitchen tables and packed boxes from the basement, enlisting the help of our loved ones wherever we could. From that little family, we've grown to include an amazing group of creative folks who love cooking, decorating and creating as much as we do.

It's hard to believe it's been over 25 years since those kitchen-table days. Today, we're best known for our homestyle, family-friendly cookbooks. We love hand-picking the recipes and are tickled to share our inspiration, ideas and more with you! One thing's for sure, we couldn't have done it without our friends all across the country. Whether you've been along for the ride from the begining or are just discovering us, welcome to our family!

Your friends at Gooseberry Patch

Find us here too!

Join our **Circle of Friends** and discover free recipes & crafts, plus giveaways & more! Visit our website or blog to join and be sure to follow us on Facebook & Twitter too.

Join our Circle of Friends

VIDEOS

Find us on Facebook

Read Our Blog

Follow us on twitter

www.gooseberrypatch.com

Menu Index

HALLOWEEN OPEN HOUSE
(PAGE 50)
Brew-Ha-Ha Punch (page 52)

A Great Pumpkin Cheese Ball (page 52)

Maple-Topped Sweet Potato Skins (page 53)

Fennel, Apple & Celery Slaw* (page 54)

Boil & Bubble Soup Cauldron (page 54)

Jack-o'-Lantern Bread (page 56)

Crustless Pumpkin Pie (page 56)

Serves 10 to 12

SPOOKTACULAR BLOCK PARTY
(PAGE 58)
Hot Mulled Cider (page 60)

Scarlet Sangria* (page 60)

Monsteroni Salad (page 61)

Goblin Dip & Bone Crackers (page 61)

Mummy Hot Dogs (page 62)

Don't-Be-A-Chicken Chili* (page 63)

Pumpkin Ice Cream (page 64)

Tangled Web Rice Pops (page 65)

Serves 10 to 12

BEWITCHING "BOO"FFET
(PAGE 66)
Dressed-Up Caramel Apples (page 145)

Bite-You-Back Pecans (page 68)

Blood Orange Martinis (page 68)

Caramelized Onion Dip (page 69)

Field Salad with Pears & Blue Cheese* (page 70)

Roast Pork with Sage & Pecan Pesto (page 70)

Sweet Potato Galette (page 72)

Green Beans Almondine (page 73)

Ginger Streusel-Topped Cheesecake (page 73)

Serves 6 to 8

MASQUERADE PARTY
(PAGE 74)
Gravedigger Martini* (page 76)

Monster Eyes (page 76)

Swampwater Punch (page 77)

Don't A'choke Dip (page 77)

Dripping Meatballs (page 78)

Forbidden & Fermented on Toast (page 78)

To-Die-For Rye Pizzas (page 78)

Skewered Morsels* (page 79)

Munchable Mice* (page 80)

Shrunken Heads (page 81)

Serves 12

*double recipe, **triple recipe

PUMPKIN PATCH PICNIC
(PAGE 84)
Spiced Lemonade (page 86)
Cranberry Waldorf Salad (page 86)
Country-Style 3-Bean Salad (page 87)
Pulled Pork Barbecue Sandwiches (page 88)
Loaded Potato Packets* (page 89)
Oozing Cherry Pies (page 90)
Pumpkin Lattes* (page 90)

Serves 8 to 10

FRIGHT NIGHT FILM FESTIVAL
(PAGE 92)
Spiced Pear Cider** (page 94)
Four Weekends of Popcorn:
Harvest Moon Caramel Corn (page 94)
Candy Corn Popcorn Balls (page 95)
Red Cinnamon Popcorn (page 95)
Nutty Popcorn Snack Mix (page 95)
Best-Ever Soft Pretzels (page 96)
Roasted Corn with Rosemary Butter (page 96)
Campfire Corn Dogs (page 97)
Shiny Red Candy Apples (page 97)

Serves 10

CREEPY COOKIE SWAP
(PAGE 98)
Frothy Orange Punch (page 100)
Chocolatey Pumpkin Cookies (page 100)
Black Cat Cut-Out Cookies (page 101)
Melted Witches (page 102)
Poisoned Pecan Squares (page 103)
Green Gobblin' Cookies (page 104)
Crescent Moons (page 104)
Ghosts in the Mud (page 105)

Serves 6 to 8

*double recipe, **triple recipe

CAULDRONLUCK
(PAGE 106)
Transylvanian Hot Toddy (page 108)
Trash Mix with Worms (page 108)
Bacon-Cheese Dip (page 109)
Crunchy Apple-Pear Salad (page 109)
Witch's Cauldron Chili (page 110)
Candy Corn Chocolate Cakes (page 110)
Cinn-ful Coffee (page 111)

Serves 6 to 8

SCARY SCHOOL PARTY
(PAGE 112)
Crunchy Batwings (page 114)
Fruit Swords with Ant Dip (page 115)
Scary Sandwich Platter:
Black Cat Grilled Cheeses (page 117)
Ham on Ghosts (page 117)
Turkey Fingers (page 117)
Spoiled Milk (page 118)
Spooky Spiderweb Cupcakes (page 119)

Serves 16 to 20

NEVER-SLUMBER PARTY
(PAGE 120)
Dinner:
Candy Apple Punch (page 122)
Fried Goo with Dracula Dip (page 122)
Sloppy Foes (page 123)
Broccoli Parmesan (page 123)
Halloween Sandwich Cookies (page 123)
Breakfast:
Hot Cocoa Supreme (page 124)
Citrusy French Toast (page 124)
Brown-Sugared Bacon (page 124)
Cheesy Hashbrown Potatoes (page 127)
Silly Yogurt Faces (page 127)

Serves 6 to 8

Project Index

Cookie Jar, 171
Creepy Crawlers, 37
Critter Jar, 174
Easy as Pie, 45
Embellish Your Door, 34
Embellished Pumpkins, 20
Entertaining Outdoors, 82
Entertaining Tips, 48
Feather Mask, 150
Fun and Games
• Beanbag Toss, 160
• Pumpkin Cutout, 161
• Treat Bucket, 159
Grinning Gourds, 40
Haunted Houses
• Graveyard House, 170
• Pumpkin Patch
House, 169
Homespun Halloween, 36
Icing Cone Goodie Bags, 173
It's a Wrap, 45
Juice-O'-Lantern, 41
Misfortunes, 171
Mum's the Word, 42
Orange Mask, 151

Painted Faces
• Ahoy, Matey!, 154
• Fluttering Butterfly, 153
• Precious Pumpkin, 153
• Purrrrfectly Pretty, 154
• Wickedly Witchy, 155
Painted Pumpkins, 16
Paper Lanterns, 176
Party Pumpkins, 24
Patterns
• Bug Costume, 156, 192
• Fairy Costume, 157, 196
• Lion Costume, 157, 195
• Tomato Costume, 156, 194
• Treat Bag Embellishments,
172, 197
Pumpkin Primer, 10
Pumpkin Towers, 38
Pumpkins Carved, 12
Set a Haunted Table, 33
Shrunken Heads, 81
Sinister Sideboard, 32
Stencils
• Bat Stencil, 18, 184
• "Boo" Welcome Mat, 37, 187

• Cat Stencil, 19, 176, 185
• Frankenstein Stencil, 183
• Ghost Face Stencil, 18, 184
• Ghost Stencil, 182
• Gravedigger Invitation, 188
• Jack-o'-Lantern Faces, 180-181
• Label for Soap Bubbles, 189
• Printable Soda Pop Labels, 191
• Printable Wine Labels, 190
• Spiderweb Stencil, 19, 186
• Spooky Cat Invitation, 189
• Witch Stencil, 18, 185
Sunny Spheres, 43
Tin Can Mummy Vases, 175
Topiary Magic, 44
Treat Bags, 172
Vellum Votives, 177
Wary Welcome, 30
Welcoming "Boo!", 37
White Mask, 151
Window Whimsy, 36
Windowbox Whimsy, 35
Unique Costumes
• Fancy Fairy, 157
• Ferociously Friendly Lion, 157

Credits

THANKS TO ALL OF THOSE WHO HELPED BREATHE LIFE INTO THIS BOOK:
Photographers: Jean Allsop, Ralph Anderson, Robbie Caponetto, Mary M. Chambliss, Van Chaplin, Gary Clark, Tina Cornett, Jennifer Davick, Joe Descoise, William Dickey, Beth Dreiling Hontzas, Emily Followill, Brian Francis, Laurey Glenn, Jamie Hadley, Lee Harrelson, Ray Kachatorian, Deborah Whitlaw Llewellyn, Meg McKinney, Art Meripol, Thomas J. Story, and Tim Street-Porter; **Stylists:** Cindy Manning Barr, Amy Burke, Buffy Hargett, Alyce Head, Mary Catherine Muir, and Katie Stoddard; **Food:** Lyda Jones Burnette, Marian Cooper Cairns, Rebecca Kracke Gordon, Norman King, Pam Lolley, Vanessa McNeil Rocchio, and Angela Sellers; **Models:** Sarah Bellinger, Adeline Cobbs, Ella Cobbs, Parker Cobbs, Allison Cox, Donny Griffeth, Dylan Griffeth, Harrison Griffeth, Ian Logue, and Abigail Logue; **Homes:** Craig and Judy Beatty, John Cobbs, and Sunny House Studio

Recipe Index

Appetizers and Snacks

A Great Pumpkin Cheese Ball, 52
Bacon-Cheese Dip, 109
Best-Ever Soft Pretzels, 96
Bite-You-Back Pecans, 68
Caramelized Onion Dip, 69
Crunchy Batwings, 114
Don't A'choke Dip, 77
Dripping Meatballs, 78
Forbidden & Fermented on
    Toast, 78
Fried Goo With Dracula Dip, 122
Fruit Swords with Ant Dip, 115
Goblin Dip & Bone Crackers, 61
Jack-o'-Lantern Bread, 56
Monster Eyes, 76
Nutty Popcorn Snack Mix, 95
Roasted Pumpkin Seeds, 143
Skewered Morsels, 79
To-Die-For Rye Pizzas, 78
Trash Mix With Worms, 108

Beverages

Blood Orange Martinis, 68
Brew-Ha-Ha Punch, 52
Candy Apple Punch, 122
Cinn-ful Coffee, 111
Frothy Orange Punch, 100
Gravedigger Martini, 76
Hot Cocoa Supreme, 124
Hot Mulled Cider, 60
Pumpkin Lattes, 90
Scarlet Sangria, 60
Spiced Lemonade, 86
Spiced Pear Cider, 94
Spoiled Milk, 118
Swampwater Punch, 77
Transylvanian Hot Toddy, 108

Candies & Confections

Brown Sugar Glaze, 100
Buttercream Frosting, 111
Candy Corn Popcorn Balls, 95
Chocolate-Dipped Spoons, 147
Chocolate Frosting, 101
Chocolate Spiderweb Treats, 146
Cute Candy Apples, 144
Double Chocolate-Covered Toffee
    Grahams, 138
Dressed-Up Caramel Apples, 145

Easy Marshmallows from Scratch, 136
Fairy Princess Wands, 142
Frosting, 130
Harvest Moon Caramel Corn, 94
Harvest Moon Lollipops, 141
Icing, 134
Marshmallow Cookie Spiders, 133
Marshmallow Pops, 132
Munchable Mice, 80
Red Cinnamon Popcorn, 95
Shiny Red Candy Apples, 97
White Meringue Ghosts, 144

Cookies

Baby Ghosts, 165
Black Cat Cut-Out Cookies, 101
Chocolatey Pumpkin Cookies, 100
Crescent Moons, 104
Ghosts in the Mud, 105
Gingerbread Mummies, 165
Green Gobblin' Cookies, 104
Halloween Sandwich Cookies, 123
Homemade Graham Crackers, 137
Melted Witches, 102
Message Cookies, 134
Peanut Masks, 166
Skinned Knees, 166
Sugar Cookie Pops, 131
Tangled Web Rice Pops, 65
Tire Tracks, 166
Tombstone Cookies, 165

Desserts

Candy Corn Chocolate Cakes, 110
Candy Corn Trifles, 164
Crustless Pumpkin Pie, 56
Ginger Streusel-Topped
    Cheesecake, 73
Ice-Cream Cone Cakes, 130
Mini Cupcake Pumpkin, 164
Ooey, Gooey S'mores, 91
Oozing Cherry Pies, 90
Poisoned Pecan Squares, 103
Pumpkin Ice Cream, 64
Scary Spiders, 166
Simon the Centipede, 135
Spooky Spiderweb Cupcakes, 119
Vampire Teeth, 167
Witches' Fingers, 167
Wizard Hats, 168

Entrées

Black Cat Grilled Cheeses, 117
Boil & Bubble Soup Cauldron, 54
Campfire Corn Dogs, 97
Citrusy French Toast, 124
Don't-Be-A-Chicken Chili, 63
Ham on Ghosts, 117
Mummy Hot Dogs, 62
Pulled Pork Barbecue Sandwiches, 88
Roast Pork with Sage & Pecan
    Pesto, 70
Sloppy Foes, 123
Turkey Fingers, 117
Witch's Cauldron Chili, 110

Salads & Dressings

Country-Style 3-Bean Salad, 87
Cranberry Waldorf Salad, 86
Crunchy Apple-Pear Salad, 109
Dressing, 109
Fennel, Apple & Celery Slaw, 54
Field Salad with Pears & Blue
    Cheese, 70
Monsteroni Salad, 61

Sauces, Condiments & Mixes

Cappuccino Waffle Mix with Coffee
    Syrup, 139
Coffee Syrup, 139
Creamy Filling, 123
Dry Rub Mix, 88
Sage & Pecan Pesto, 71
Simple Syrup, 68

Side Dishes

Broccoli Parmesan, 123
Brown-Sugared Bacon, 124
Cheesy Hashbrown Potatoes, 127
Green Beans Almondine, 73
Loaded Potato Packets, 89
Maple-Topped Sweet Potato Skins, 53
Roasted Corn With Rosemary
    Butter, 96
Silly Yogurt Faces, 127
Sweet Potato Galette, 72

METRIC EQUIVALENTS

The recipes that appear in this cookbook use the standard U.S. method for measuring liquid and dry or solid ingredients (teaspoons, tablespoons, and cups). The information in the following charts is provided to help cooks outside the United States successfully use these recipes. All equivalents are approximate.

METRIC EQUIVALENTS FOR DIFFERENT TYPES OF INGREDIENTS

A standard cup measure of a dry or solid ingredient will vary in weight depending on the type of ingredient.
A standard cup of liquid is the same volume for any type of liquid. Use the following chart when converting standard cup measures to grams (weight) or milliliters (volume).

Standard Cup	Fine Powder (ex. flour)	Grain (ex. rice)	Granular (ex. sugar)	Liquid Solids (ex. butter)	Liquid (ex. milk)
1	140 g	150 g	190 g	200 g	240 ml
3/4	105 g	113 g	143 g	150 g	180 ml
2/3	93 g	100 g	125 g	133 g	160 ml
1/2	70 g	75 g	95 g	100 g	120 ml
1/3	47 g	50 g	63 g	67 g	80 ml
1/4	35 g	38 g	48 g	50 g	60 ml
1/8	18 g	19 g	24 g	25 g	30 ml

USEFUL EQUIVALENTS FOR LIQUID INGREDIENTS BY VOLUME

1/4 tsp	=				1 ml
1/2 tsp	=				2 ml
1 tsp	=				5 ml
3 tsp	= 1 tbls		= 1/2 fl oz	=	15 ml
	2 tbls	= 1/8 cup	= 1 fl oz	=	30 ml
	4 tbls	= 1/4 cup	= 2 fl oz	=	60 ml
	5 1/3 tbls	= 1/3 cup	= 3 fl oz	=	80 ml
	8 tbls	= 1/2 cup	= 4 fl oz	=	120 ml
	10 2/3 tbls	= 2/3 cup	= 5 fl oz	=	160 ml
	12 tbls	= 3/4 cup	= 6 fl oz	=	180 ml
	16 tbls	= 1 cup	= 8 fl oz	=	240 ml
1 pt	= 2 cups	= 16 fl oz	=		480 ml
1 qt	= 4 cups	= 32 fl oz	=		960 ml
		= 33 fl oz	= 1000 ml = 1 liter		

USEFUL EQUIVALENTS FOR DRY INGREDIENTS BY WEIGHT

(To convert ounces to grams, multiply the number of ounces by 30.)

1 oz	=	1/16 lb	=	30 g
4 oz	=	1/4 lb	=	120 g
8 oz	=	1/2 lb	=	240 g
12 oz	=	3/4 lb	=	360 g
16 oz	=	1 lb	=	480 g

USEFUL EQUIVALENTS FOR LENGTH

(To convert inches to centimeters, multiply the number of inches by 2.5.)

1 in =			= 2.5 cm	
6 in =	1/2 ft		= 15 cm	
12 in =	1 ft		= 30 cm	
36 in =	3 ft	= 1 yd	= 90 cm	
40 in =			= 100 cm	= 1 meter

USEFUL EQUIVALENTS FOR COOKING/OVEN TEMPERATURES

	Fahrenheit	Celsius	Gas Mark
Freeze Water	32° F	0° C	
Room Temperature	68° F	20° C	
Boil Water	212° F	100° C	
Bake	325° F	160° C	3
	350° F	180° C	4
	375° F	190° C	5
	400° F	200° C	6
	425° F	220° C	7
	450° F	230° C	8
Broil			Grill

THE END

【 *Gone to rest in the Gooseberry Patch.* 】